A HISTORY OF
THE AMERICAN PEOPLE

BY

WOODROW WILSON, Ph.D., Litt.D., LL.D.

IN FIVE VOLUMES

VOL. V.

Reunion and Nationalization

A HISTORY OF
THE AMERICAN PEOPLE

BY

WOODROW WILSON, Ph.D., Litt.D., LL.D.

PRESIDENT OF PRINCETON UNIVERSITY

ILLUSTRATED WITH PORTRAITS, MAPS
PLANS, FACSIMILES, RARE PRINTS
CONTEMPORARY VIEWS, ETC.

IN FIVE VOLUMES

VOL. V.

NEW YORK AND LONDON
HARPER & BROTHERS PUBLISHERS
MCMIII

3330

CONTENTS

NOTES ON ILLUSTRATIONS

NOTES ON ILLUSTRATIONS

NOTES ON ILLUSTRATIONS

NOTES ON ILLUSTRATIONS

NOTES ON ILLUSTRATIONS

xi

NOTES ON ILLUSTRATIONS

LIST OF MAPS

A HISTORY
OF THE AMERICAN PEOPLE

A HISTORY
OF THE AMERICAN PEOPLE

CHAPTER I

RECONSTRUCTION

MR. LINCOLN'S death made Mr. Johnson President.
The first tasks of peace were to be hardly less difficult
than the tasks of war had been; and the party which
had triumphed was left without executive leadership
at their very beginning. Mr. Johnson was a man who,
like Mr. Lincoln himself, had risen from very humble
origins to posts of trust and distinction; but his coarse
fibre had taken no polish, no refinement in the process.
He stopped neither to understand nor to persuade other
men, but struck forward with crude, uncompromising
force for his object, attempting mastery without wisdom
or moderation. Wisdom of no common order was called
for in the tasks immediately before him. What effect
had the war wrought upon the federal system? What
was now the status of the States which had attempted
secession and been brought to terms only by two million
armed men sent into the field and the pouring out of
blood and treasure beyond all reckoning? Were they
again States of the Union, or had they forfeited their

statehood and become conquered provinces merely, to be dealt with at the will of Congress? If conquered possessions, how and when were they to be made States once more and the old federal circle restored in its integrity? Mr. Lincoln had made up his mind upon these points with characteristic directness and simplicity. So long ago as December, 1863, he had issued a proclamation of amnesty in which he had treated secession as a rebellion of individuals, not of States, and had offered full forgetfulness and the restoration of property and of citizenship to all who should take oath to "support, protect, and defend the constitution of the United States and the union of the States thereunder," and respect the action of the federal government in the emancipation of the slaves. Some classes of persons he excepted from the amnesty: those who had taken a prominent and official part in secession or who had left the service of the United States for the service of the Confederacy; but he invited those who would take the oath proposed to set up governments once more and make ready to take part as of old in the federal system, though they should number but one tenth of the voters of 1860. The qualified voters of Arkansas, Louisiana, and Tennessee had accepted these terms before the war ended. Mr. Lincoln had fulfilled his promise to them and given full recognition to the new governments they set up, so far as the Executive was concerned, as once more in their places in the Union. He did not stop to discuss the question of the lawyers, whether these States had been all the while in the Union, despite their attempts at secession and their acts of war against the federal government, or had for a time been out of it; and declared that he thought that

2

merely an abstract inquiry, a question practically immaterial. "We all agree that the seceded States, so
called, are out of their proper practical relation with the
Union," he said, "and that the sole object of the government, civil and military, in regard to those States
is to again get them into that proper practical relation.
I believe that it is not only possible, but in fact easier,
to do this without deciding or even considering whether
these States have been out of the Union, than with it.
Finding themselves safely at home, it would be utterly
immaterial whether they had ever been abroad."

But Congress had not acquiesced in Mr. Lincoln's
policy. Mr. Lincoln had been too much inclined, it
seemed to the leaders of the houses, to regard the
restoration of the southern States to their "proper practical relation to the Union" as a matter to be settled by
the action of the Executive. The constitution made
each house the sole judge of the validity of elections to its
membership: Congress was at liberty, should it choose,
to exclude all southern members until it should itself
be satisfied with the process by which the States they
claimed to represent had been re-established upon their
old footing; and the temper of the congressional leaders
had grown more and more radical as the fortunes of
war had turned their doubt into hope, their hope into
triumphant confidence. At first they had been puzzled
how to read the law of the constitution in so unprecedented a matter; but each victory in arms had seemed
to them to make it less necessary that they should read
it with subtlety. Success seemed to clear the way
for other considerations, of plainer dictate than the
law of the constitution. Turn the matter this way or
that, it seemed mere weakness to accord the southern

3

States their old place in the Union without exacting of them something more than mere submission. Should their social system be left untouched, their old life and power given back to them to be used as before for the perpetuation of political beliefs and domestic institutions which had in fact lain at the heart of the war? Opinion slowly gathered head to prevent any such course. Something should be demanded of them which should make them like the rest of the Union, not in allegiance merely, but in principle and practice as well.

Mr. Lincoln had himself made it a condition precedent to his recognition of the re-established liberties and allegiance of those southerners whom he was ready to permit to bring their States into proper practical relation with the Union again that the laws of the rehabilitated governments should "recognize and declare the permanent freedom" of the negroes and provide for their education; no one, North or South, dreamed that slavery was to be set up again. But every man mistook his feeling for principle in that day of heat, and Mr. Lincoln's cool, judicial tone and purpose in affairs was deeply disquieting to all who loved drastic action. The solemn, sweet-tempered sentences with which his second inaugural address had closed seemed themselves of bad omen to high-strung men. "With malice towards none; with charity for all; with firmness in the right, as God gives us to see the right, let us strive on to finish the work we are in; to bind up the nation's wounds; . . . to do all which may achieve and cherish a just and lasting peace among ourselves, and with all nations." In the proclamation in which he had called upon all who were willing to return to their allegiance in the South to reconstruct their governments he had promised that, as President, he would object to no temporary legislation which should deal

Henry Wilson   HENRY WILSON

in exceptional fashion with the negroes "as a laboring, landless, homeless class" for a little while under tutelage, provided only their substantial freedom should be recognized and their ultimate elevation by education provided for. There was in all this entirely too much consideration for the southern people to suit the views of ordinary partisans. An opposition gathered head against Mr. Lincoln which it seemed likely even his tact, his genius for leadership and conciliation, his authority in that day of his final prestige could not overcome.

Men of many minds and of all morals were arrayed against him: the philanthropist and the reformer, who saw the Rights of Man involved, the statesman who wished to see the ground once for all cleared of every matter of risk and controversy, the politician who was keen to gain the utmost advantage for his party, the vindictive bigot who wished to wreak exemplary vengeance on the slaveholding rebels. To many of these nothing was so exasperating as moderation,—moderation in a day of absolute triumph, when every fruit of conquest they chose to stretch out their hands and pluck was within their easy reach. It was not an air in which to judge calmly. Four years of doubt and fear and struggle had wrought every sentiment, good or bad, to the pitch of ecstasy. A radical course of reconstruction in the South had come to look like the mere path of duty,—of duty not to opinion only but to mankind as well. Men of imagination felt every moment of action dramatic, full of consequence, and grew self-conscious, each as it were with a touch of the emotional actor, in what they did. The extraordinary strain and tension of feeling in the houses of Congress was perceptible to mere lookers on in the galleries. It had been notably manifest when the House of Representatives agreed, on the last day of January, 1865, to an amendment of the constitution formally abolishing slavery in the very terms of the

6

Wilmot proviso, and the celebrated Ordinance of 1787 upon which so much bitter history had turned. The Senate had proposed the amendment, the Thirteenth it was to be,—the first change in the constitution proposed since 1803,—ten months before, on the 8th of April, 1864; but the necessary two-thirds vote had been lacking then in the House and it had been laid aside. When it came a second time to the vote a deathly stillness prevailed in the House while the roll call proceeded, until it became evident that the requisite majority was secured. Then members of the House itself broke through all restraint and joined in the great shout of joy that went up from the packed galleries, and embraced one another, with tears streaming down their cheeks, to see that prayed for end come at last. Men dreamed, as they had dreamed in the Constituent Assembly of France, that they had that day seen a new nation born, a new era ushered in.

Congress had already abolished slavery in the District of Columbia, prohibited slavery in the Territories, repealed the Fugitive Slave Law, and bestowed freedom upon the negroes who had served in the federal armies. The amendment was to complete the work of emancipation, and make the results of the war once for all safe against reaction. The votes of the southern States were necessary to make up the three-fourths vote of the States required to ratify the amendment. Those which accepted Mr. Lincoln's terms of rehabilitation ratified it without hesitation: no one doubted that a condition precedent to the final closing of the long strife that had rent the Union; and on the 18th of December, 1865, it was proclaimed an integral part of the law of the constitution.

7

But there were men in Congress, true spokesmen of thousands of men out-of-doors, thoughtful and thought-less, with consciences and without, who meant to go much further. By some means they meant to thrust their hands into southern affairs to control them, to make good the freedom and the privilege of the negroes even at the cost of all privilege to those who had been their masters. To some such a course seemed a mere dictate of humanity: the nation owed it to the negro that he should be supported by the federal power until he was able to make his freedom good for himself, un-assisted. To others it seemed but the plain way of prudence in statesmanship. How else could a lasting structure of law be built about the new citizenship of the one-time slave: how else could he be kept safe from the intellectual and even physical domination of the white men who once had owned him? To others it was the course of personal satisfaction: in no other way could they bring upon the spirits of southern men the punishment merited by their rebellion. To others it was the obvious means of party mastery. These last it was who, when Mr. Lincoln was gone, ruled Congress, the masters of party strategy,—as clear of their motive as Samuel Adams, as astute to veil it upon occasion: masters always by consistent and aggressive force of purpose.

The party they spoke for was not one of the historic parties of the Union. It was the child of the slavery contest. It had come into existence, an odd mixture of Whigs, Democrats, Free Soilers, Anti-Nebraska men, to prevent the spread of slavery into the Terri-tories, and had come into power with a programme which spoke, indeed, of other matters, with a tone which was chiefly the tone of the older Whigs, but which carried as its chief, its creative principle that single matter of the restriction of the slave power. It was without record or tradition of ordinary service in times of normal life and growth. Its single task had been war for the preservation of the Union. It could not of a sudden get the temper of that task out of its thoughts; conciliation it had never learned; compromise and accommodation seemed to it bad things of a past age when men were not bold for the right. Mr. Thaddeus Stevens, of Pennsylvania, was the real leader of the House. He had come slowly to his final view of what should be done, acted upon by the times and the confused voices of counsel about him, as every man was in that shifting air, but he had reached conclusions at last which he spoke with callous frankness. In his judgment, he said, the southern States "ought never to be recognized as capable of acting in the Union, or of being recognized as valid states, until the Constitution should have been so amended as to make it what its makers intended, and so as to secure perpetual ascendency to the party of the Union." The perpetual ascendency of his party was, in his programme, to be the guarantee of the safe reconstruction of the southern governments.

The events of the memorable summer of 1865 had hardened his temper to that view. At first Mr. Johnson had seemed to the radical leaders of Congress a man to their own mind. His origin, his character, his place of leadership among the southern men who had doggedly set themselves against secession, had made him a fit instrument of radical action. He came of plebeian stock; had risen, not by address, but by blunt force of character, from among the humbler whites who owned no slaves, boasted no privilege, had no initiative voice in affairs; and had flung himself on the side of the Union as much out of antagonism to the men who played the parts of leadership in secession as out of principle. It was "a rich man's war," he said, "but a poor man's fight"; and he, for one, would not fight for the behoof of the rich planters who assumed the mastery in such a struggle. A "Democrat" he was still, by cast and nature committed to the elder doctrines of the Jeffersonian creed, which exalted the common man and knew no rank or privilege of class; but a Democrat for the Union. He had been put upon the presidential ticket with Mr. Lincoln because upon every question that touched the war the Republican leaders had wished to keep men of all opinions upon other matters of policy united behind Mr. Lincoln. His short and heavy figure, his rugged, swarthy face, bespoke him a man as strong, as indomitable as Stephen Douglas, for all he lacked Douglas's charm and had no gift of persuasion.

Mr. Lincoln had trusted him, and he had justified the confidence reposed in him, not indeed by wisdom, but by resolute, consistent, efficient action. When the war came he was one of the senators from Tennessee, and kept his post, ignoring the secession of his State. When his term as senator was ended Tennessee was in the hands of the federal troops, and Mr. Lincoln commissioned him military governor of the State, to bring it again into "proper practical relation to the Union" in accordance with the Executive's plan of reconstruction. Like every man, untouched with greatness, who has stood out against his own people in matters that have been carried the length of civil war, there was a dash of bitterness in Mr. Johnson's attitude and action in affairs. The first words he uttered as President showed with what spirit he meant to use his new power. "The American people," he said, "must be taught to know and understand that treason is a crime. . . . It must not be regarded as a mere difference of political opinion. It must not be excused as an unsuccessful rebellion, to be overlooked and forgiven." The Committee on the Conduct of the War, to which Congress had throughout the stress of the fighting intrusted the shaping of its business, called upon him the day following his assumption of the presidency, and took heart to believe after their interview with him that they might count upon such executive action as radicals would relish,—that they were once for all rid of the mild counsels of Mr. Lincoln. "Johnson, we have faith in you," cried Mr. Benjamin Wade, the radical leader of the Senate. "By the gods! there will be no trouble now in running the government."

But a few weeks changed the whole aspect of affairs. Mr. Johnson retained Mr. Lincoln's cabinet unchanged. More than that, he kept to the plans Mr. Lincoln had made. Perhaps his judgment was cleared by sudden access of responsibility; no doubt his knowledge of the southern people enabled him to see, more clearly even than Mr. Lincoln had seen, the healing and beneficent effects of a plan of reconstruction which should make as little of the antagonism and as much of the community of interest between the sections as possible: for he acted upon experience, Mr. Lincoln only upon the instinct of a natural leader of men. No doubt men whom he trusted gave him moderate counsel and instructed his will. Whatever the forces that ruled him, he proved at once that he meant to take no radical course of his own, but would follow in Mr. Lincoln's footsteps. On the 29th of May he issued his own proclamation of amnesty. Its terms were substantially the terms

BENJAMIN FRANKLIN WADE

of Mr. Lincoln's proclamation of 1863. The list of those excluded for the time being was a little extended. Besides persons still prisoners of war, those who had "held the pretended offices of governors of States in insurrection against the United States," graduates of

12

the military and naval academies who had been officers
in the confederate service, those who had engaged in
the destruction of the commerce of the United States
in aid of the Confederacy,—whom Mr. Lincoln had
not specifically included in his catalogue of exclusions,
—he added, as if to please himself and satisfy his instinct of class, all participants in secession whose taxable
property exceeded twenty thousand dollars in value.
But even to those thus specifically excepted he promised
to extend clemency upon very liberal terms, if they
would make personal application for it, dealing with
them in as generous a manner as might seem "consistent with the facts of the case and the peace and
dignity of the United States."

It was his plan, as it had been Mr. Lincoln's, to set
up new governments in the South by as simple and
expeditious a process as possible. He knew as well
as any man the practical details of what Mr. Lincoln
had meant to do, for he had himself been Mr. Lincoln's agent in putting his plan of reconstruction
into execution in Tennessee. Each State was to have a
provisional governor, appointed by the President, who
should be authorized to summon a constitutional convention, to be chosen under its old laws of suffrage by
such of the voters of the State as would take the unqualified oath of submission and allegiance prescribed
by the proclamation of amnesty. It had been Mr.
Lincoln's wish to include among the voters such freedmen as could read and write and those who had served
in the federal armies; Mr. Johnson confined his view
to the white men qualified under the laws of their States
as they had stood in the spring of 1861. Conventions
made up of and selected by those who were willing

13

and were permitted to take the oath offered were to be given full power to recast their state constitutions and set their state governments in order for the final withdrawal of the federal troops and the federal superintendence, provided only that the voters actually enrolled should number at least one tenth of the total number shown upon the rolls of 1861. The persons explicitly excluded from taking the oath and participating in the reconstitution of the southern governments,—those who had been the leading spirits and chief agents of the Confederacy, whether in counsel or in action,—were, of course, the leading men of the South. Almost no one could take the oath of amnesty except men of the rank and file, the men who had not been slaveholders, who had fought in the armies of the Confederacy but who had had no part except the part of mere acquiescence in bringing the war on,—the men of little property and no leading part in affairs from whose ranks Mr. Johnson himself had sprung. His added exclusion of all participants in secession who owned property valued at more than twenty thousand dollars made it the more certain that it should be a reconstruction by the third estate, and not by the old leaders of opinion. He had the greater heart and interest on that account to see the plan succeed.

He had come into office at the beginning of the long congressional recess. The term of the Congress chosen in 1862 had expired on the 4th of March; the Congress chosen in the autumn of 1864 was not to come together until December. He had eight months before him in which to act without congressional interference. He was urged to call the houses together in extraordinary session and take counsel with them what should be done; but he refused to do so. He wished to act without restraint. He had no more doubt than Mr. Lincoln had had that the process of reconstruction, so far as it concerned the reorganization of the southern governments, was the function and the duty of the Executive,

ANDREW JOHNSON

whose power of pardon covered every offence committed against the Union upon which Congress had not passed sentence of impeachment. It rested with Congress, he knew, to determine for itself whether it would receive the senators and representatives chosen under the governments which the President should authorize

15

the southern conventions to set up; but the erection and recognition of those governments he conceived to be his own unquestionable constitutional prerogative. He filled the year, therefore, to the utmost with action and the rehabilitation of States. By the autumn every State of the one-time Confederacy had acted under his proclamation, had set up a new government, had formally agreed to the emancipation of the negroes, and had chosen senators and representatives ready to take their seats the moment Congress should admit them. Eleven of them had in due form adopted the Thirteenth Amendment, and their votes had been counted in its ratification.

But other things had happened which had touched Congress quite as nearly as these processes of reconstruction, and the houses came together in December in no temper either to accept Mr. Johnson's leadership or to admit the southern members who had come to Washington under his patronage. Critical matters touching the negroes had put opinion in the North in a mood to insist on radical measures of legislation in behalf of the helpless multitudes whom the war had set free. Had there been no question what should be done with the negroes, all might have gone smoothly enough, whether the leaders of Congress and of opinion liked the re-admission of the southerners to their place and privilege in the general government or not. But there was much more to be done, as it seemed to the radicals who now stood at the front of counsel, than merely to determine the processes by which the governments of the southern States were to be formally reconstituted and made safe within the Union: and it was no doubt necessary to do what was to be done before admitting southern men to Congress, where their presence would reduce the Republican majorities from absolute mastery to mere preponderance. They were but "whitewashed rebels," at best, and in nothing showed their unchanged temper more clearly than in their treatment of the freedmen. That, in the view of the radicals, was the crux of the whole matter; and they had the pity and the humane feeling of the whole country on their side.

They did not deem the southerners safe friends of the freed slaves. They had not noted how quiet, how unexcited, how faithful and steady at their accustomed tasks, how devoted in the service of their masters the great mass of the negro people had remained amidst the very storm and upheaval of war; they had noted only how thousands had crowded into their camps as the armies advanced and plantations were laid waste, homes emptied of their inmates; and how every federal commander had had to lead in his train as he moved a dusky host of pitiful refugees. It was a mere act of imperative mercy to care in some sort for the helpless creatures, to give them food, if nothing else, out of the army's stores; and yet to feed them was but to increase their numbers, as the news of bread without work spread through the country-sides. When the fighting neared its end, and it was likely that the whole South would be in the hands of the federal commanders through a long season of unsettled affairs, it became obviously necessary that, for a time at least, Congress should take the negroes under the direct supervision and care of the government. On the 3d of March, 1865, therefore, while Mr. Lincoln still lived, an Act had been passed which created in the War Department a "Bureau of Refugees, Freedmen, and Abandoned Lands," whose powers were most elastic and paternal. It was in every way to succor the negroes: to supply their physical needs when necessary, to act as their representative and guardian in finding employment and making labor contracts, to settle labor disputes and act as the next friend of negro litigants in all trials and suits at law, to lease to them tracts of abandoned land temporarily in the hands of the government because of the removal or disappearance or technical outlawry of their white owners,—in all things to supply them with privilege and protection.

It was such aid and providential succor the negroes had ignorantly looked for as the news and vision of emancipation spread amongst them with the progress of the war. They had dreamed that the blue-coated armies which stormed slowly southward were bringing them, not freedom only, but largess of fortune as well; and now their dream seemed fulfilled. The government would find land for them, would feed them and give them clothes. It would find work for them, but it did not seem to matter whether work was found or not: they would be taken care of. They had the easy faith, the simplicity, the idle hopes, the inexperience of children. Their masterless, homeless freedom made them the more pitiable, the more dependent, because under slavery they had been shielded, the weak and incompetent with the strong and capable; had never learned independence or the rough buffets of freedom.

The southern legislatures which Mr. Johnson authorized set up saw the need for action no less than Congress did. It was a menace to society itself that the negroes should thus of a sudden be set free and left without tutelage or restraint. Some stayed very

18

quietly by their old masters and gave no trouble; but most yielded, as was to have been expected, to the novel impulse and excitement of freedom and made their

Edwin M. Stanton

EDWIN McMASTERS STANTON

way straight to the camps and cities, where the blue-coated soldiers were, and the agents of the Freedmen's Bureau. The country filled with vagrants, looking for pleasure and gratuitous fortune. Idleness bred want, as always, and the vagrants turned thieves or importunate beggars. The tasks of ordinary labor stood untouched; the idlers grew insolent, dangerous; nights went anxiously by, for fear of riot and incendiary fire. It was imperatively necessary that something should be done, if only to bring order again and make the streets of the towns and the highways of the country-sides safe to those who went about their tasks. The southern legislatures, therefore, promptly undertook remedies of their own,—such remedies as English legislators had been familiar with time out of mind.

The vagrants, it was enacted, should be bound out to compulsory labor; and all who would not work must be treated as vagrants. Written contracts of labor were required, and current rates of wages were prescribed. Those who did not enter into formal contracts for regular employment were obliged to obtain licenses for their trades and occupations from the magistrates or the police authorities of their places of labor, under the penalty of falling under the law of vagrancy. Minor negroes were to be put under masters by articles of apprenticeship. Negroes were forbidden, upon pain of arrest by a vigilant patrol, to be abroad after the ringing of the curfew at nine o'clock, without written permission from their employers. Fines were ordered for a numerous list of the more annoying minor offences likely to be committed by the freedmen, and it was directed that those who could not pay the fines should be hired out to labor by judicial process. There was no concert or uniformity between State and State in the measures adopted: some were more harsh and radical than others. Each State acted according to the apparent exigencies and circumstances of its own people. Where the negroes mustered in largest numbers, as in South

Carolina, where they outnumbered the whites, restriction was, of course, pushed farthest and the most thorough-going legal tutelage for the freedmen attempted. Where their numbers were more manageable, where conditions were more favorable, their freedom of movement and of occupation was less interfered with.

There was nothing unprecedented in such legislation, even where it went farthest. The greater part of it was paralleled by statutes of labor and vagrancy still to be found on the statute books of several of the northern States. But it was impossible it should stand in the same light. The labor and vagrancy laws of Maine, Rhode Island, and Connecticut, which they most resembled, were uttered against a few tramps and beggars, here and there a runaway servant or apprentice, an occasional breach of duties regularly contracted for; while these new laws of the South were uttered against an entire race, but just now emancipated. Whatever their justification, it was inevitable that they should shock the sentiment of the North and make new and bitter enemies for the South in Congress. It was no ordinary time of action, when matters could be judged coolly and on their merits. For the leaders of Congress it was unpalatable enough that the southern States should have legislatures at all, upon a plan made and executed without conference with them; that those legislatures should thus undo the work of emancipation seemed a thing intolerable. And the new legislation seemed to them nothing less than that. It seemed to them merely an effort to substitute compulsory contracts of service and fixed rates of wages for the older rights of control and duties of support which custom

21

had vouchsafed and assigned masters of slaves,—a sort of involuntary servitude by judicial process and under the forms of contract. They did not stop to consider the pressing necessity or the extraordinary circumstances which justified such legislation. There were many theories held among them as to the legal powers and remaining rights of the southern States, but their purpose of mastery in the readjustment of southern affairs was not materially affected by their differing theories. They in effect regarded the southern States as conquered provinces, and looked upon emancipation as the main fruit of conquest. To make that emancipation good was only to secure the conquest itself. The negro had got a veritable apotheosis in the minds of northern men by the processes of the war. Those who had sent their sons to the field of battle to die in order that he might be free could but regard him as the innocent victim of circumstances, a creature who needed only liberty to make him a man; could but regard any further attempt on the part of his one-time masters to restrain him as mere vindictive defiance. They did not look into the facts: they let their sentiment and their sense of power dictate their thought and purpose.

Neither was it any part of the case, so far as they and their leaders in Congress were concerned, that the restrictive legislation which they so bitterly resented had been practically without effect, because virtually set aside by the action of the Freedmen's Bureau. Everywhere throughout the South agents of the Bureau practically made the law which should in fact govern the negro and determine his relation to his employer. It was a Bureau of the War Department; its head was a general of the army; and its agents were for the most part army officers. In many instances they were men of fine purpose and unimpeachable integrity, manly and anxious to do what was right and just to all concerned; but in many other instances they were men of petty temper, fond of using arbitrary power very masterfully, and glad upon occasion to use it for the utter humiliation of the southern white men with whom they dealt. Sometimes they were actually corrupt, and apt at every practice which promised them either added authority or private gain. Their powers, under the Act of Congress, were in effect unlimited. They interfered with the processes of the courts; constituted themselves judges of every matter, whether of law or policy, that affected the negroes; made contracts for them and released them from their obligations at will; prescribed the services they should render and the wages they should receive; ignored and set at naught every provision of state law which touched the action or the privileges of the freedmen; and, for good or ill, to fulfil their duty or to please themselves, were masters of the situation.

But that was what the congressional leaders had planned and expected. It did not lessen their irritation that the southern legislators had been in large part unsuccessful in what they had attempted to do. When at last the long recess was over, therefore, and the houses once more assembled (December 4, 1865), it at once became evident that they had come together in a mood to insist upon their own way of settling southern affairs. The names of all the States that had seceded were omitted in the roll call. As soon as possible after the organization of the House, a joint committee of fifteen, consisting

23

of nine representatives and six senators, was set up
to take charge of the business of the houses in the matter of reconstruction. It was commissioned to make
thorough inquiry into the condition of affairs at the
South and to advise Congress what action it should
take with regard to the readmission of the southern
States to representation. There was no need that
it should be in haste to report. The houses had already in effect adopted the view of Mr. Thaddeus
Stevens: that the secession of the southern States had
suspended all federal law, whether of the constitution
or of statute, so far as they were concerned; that only
the law-making and war-making branch of the federal
government, the Congress itself, could authoritatively
declare that law in force again; and that it might and
should refuse to do so until itself satisfied of the absolute
submission and unqualified obedience of the rebellious
communities. There was every reason, if the President
meant to stand in its way, why Congress should keep
for the present its omnipotent party majorities. Each
house, as it stood, had a Republican majority large
enough, and compact enough, if it came to a struggle
with the President, to override any veto he might venture
to interpose to check its action. Should the southern
States be readmitted to representation as they stood,
under the President's reconstruction, they would quite
certainly send Democratic members to swell the ranks
of the party which had, in its convention of 1864, declared
the war a failure, and would rob the war party of its
predominance. For they must be accorded an increased
representation. The slaves, now that they were free,
must all be counted in apportioning representation;
and yet the whites only would vote. It was that view

of the future of party politics that had led Mr. Sumner to declare, even before the actual struggle of the war was over, that "the cause of human rights and of the Union needed the ballots as well as the muskets of the

Thaddeus Stevens   THADDEUS STEVENS

colored men"; and the leaders of the houses had no mind to yield their complete power until they had won their final ascendency.

In February, 1866, their Committee on Reconstruction safely in the saddle, they found themselves in direct conflict with the President, and the fight for which they had made ready begun. The Act of March, 1865, which had established the Freedmen's Bureau, had limited its operation to one year. On the 6th of February, 1866, a bill passed the houses continuing it indefinitely, and at the same time largely increasing its powers. It made any attempt to obstruct, interfere with, or abridge the civil rights and immunities of the freedmen a penal offence, to be adjudged and punished by federal military tribunals. The President vetoed it. He declared that he withheld his assent both because the measure was calculated to increase the restlessness and uneasiness of the negroes and delay their settlement to a normal way of life, and because it had been passed by a Congress in which the southern States were not represented; and so joined issue directly with the men who had set the houses in a way of mastery. An attempt to pass the bill over his veto failed. The full party vote was not yet at the command of the radicals; some still held off from an open and final breach with the President.

But not for long. The President was in a mood as bitter and defiant as that of the extremest radical of the congressional majority. By sheer rashness and intemperance he forced the consolidation of the majority against him. In a public speech uttered on the 22d of February, an anniversary of hope and good omen, he spoke of the majority in unmeasured terms of denunciation, and of its leaders by name, as men who themselves entertained some covert purpose of disloyalty to the government, planning to make it a government, not federal, but consolidated and unlimited in power,—it might be even encouraging some criminal deed against himself such as had once already removed an obstacle from the path of their ambition. Accommodation between himself and the houses was once for all impossible. It was as if he had openly declared war upon them; and their temper hardened to crush

ULYSSES SIMPSON GRANT, ABOUT 1867

him. Though the effort to pass the bill for the continuation of the Freedmen's Bureau had failed in the Senate, the houses had in their very hour of failure sent to the President and published to the country a concurrent resolution in which they announced that no senator or representative would be admitted from any State held to have been in insurrection until Congress had upon its own terms and initiative declared it entitled to representation. Having heard his bitter speech of the 22d, they moved forward to execute the programme of their Committee on Reconstruction with a new spirit of mastery.

In March they sent to the President a "Civil Rights" bill which declared "all persons born in the United States, and not subject to any foreign power," citizens of the United States; denounced severe penalties against interference with the civil rights of any class of citizens; and gave to officers of the United States the right to prosecute, to the courts of the United States the exclusive right to try, all such offences,—meaning thus to put the negroes upon a footing of civil equality with the whites in the South. The President vetoed the bill, as both unwise and in plain excess of the constitutional powers of Congress. In April, the houses passed it over his veto. The same month their Committee, as if less confident of their constitutional ground than of their parliamentary supremacy, submitted the draft of a Fourteenth Amendment to the constitution which should embody the principles of the Act in a form which would give. them unalterable validity. It conferred citizenship in the terms of the bill the President had rejected. In June Congress adopted the Amendment, and it went to the States, with the understanding that no southern State which did not accept it should be readmitted to representation. Tennessee promptly adopted it, and in July was formally reinstated in her "former proper practical relation to the Union" by the admission of her senators and representatives to Congress. Her case stood apart from the rest. Ever since Mr. Lincoln's proclamation of 1863 was put into effect she had been in process of reorganization. She had gone doubting and divided into the Confederacy, more than half her people, it might be, still staunchly minded to stand by the Union. Her "Union men" had controlled the process of reconstruction; and were heeded without serious difficulty when they knocked for admission into the houses. The other States, being as yet in other hands, were obliged to wait.

The troubled year went uneasily upon every hand. As the spring came on, and all the country saw how it had come to an open breach between the President and Congress, movements began on the Canadian frontier which discovered a new disturbing element in international politics. While the war lasted New York had become the seat of the offices of a great society of Irishmen whose purpose was revolution over sea and that liberation of Ireland which Irishmen had ever prayed for. Across the sea, in Ireland, it was an association of peasants, not of politicians: it held a rank and file, not of agitators, but of plain, unsophisticated, earnest men on its rolls, men who might be taken to stand for the mass of Irish Catholics. In America it grew strong and drank of the spirit of war from the thousands of Irish-American soldiers who served as enthusiastically in the execution of its plans as in the battles for the preservation of the Union. Servant girls, cab drivers, porters, laborers on the railways filled its treasury out of their scant earnings. "Fenian," the name it bore, was said to have been the name of the ancient Celtic militia of the emerald isle from which no true Irishman ever really tore his heart entirely away. Every man who looked below the surface of affairs believed that some day the secret of this great organization would spring to light in some burst of revolution which would shake Ireland with the rising of a whole people; and the close of the war for the Union seemed the time it had sought for a release of its power. Its first sally was not in Ireland, but in America,—across the northern border, against the English empire in Canada. It proved a thing to smile at after it was over: a few hun-

THE FENIAN RAID IN CANADA. RUINS OF FORT ERIE

dred men attempting a set invasion; a fort here and there set upon by a handful of reckless adventurers; quick defeat, repulse, dispersion. It was no slight cause of irritation to Canada, none the less, and to the English government over sea that these foolhardy foes should come from the territory of a friendly power to attempt their purpose. The government at Washington seemed singularly indifferent; did little that was effective to check the criminal business; was apparently helpless against a handful of outlaws. A touch of tragedy was added to the perplexities of politics.

30

BRITISH FLAG CAPTURED BY THE FENIANS

There was tragedy enough in the domestic situation; but it was a moral tragedy, not the tragedy of bloody raids upon a peaceful border. It was impossible to come to an understanding with Mr. Johnson. A more moderate, more approachable, more sagacious, less headstrong man might by conference have hit upon some plan by which his differences with the leaders in Congress would have been accommodated and at least a *modus vivendi* devised. But to differ with Mr. Johnson was to make an enemy of him, and Congress had suspected him an opponent rather than a friend from the first and was disinclined to seek accommodation. His intemperate fashion of speech exaggerated his views in the mere statement; he seemed a violent partisan when he wished merely to enforce a conviction or make a resolute purpose plain. Mr. Sumner came away from an interview with him convinced that he had spoken with a man who heartily despised the entire North, felt a genuine contempt for its sentiments, and meant to serve the South as entirely, as openly, as illegally as Mr. Jefferson Davis himself. What was quite as bad, the South itself got wind of his partisan temper in its behalf, nursed the false hope that it would be shielded by his power, and deepened all the mischief by acting on the hope.

It was no time at which to defy northern opinion and strengthen the hands of Congress by resistance. The autumn of the year was to bring another congressional election, and the leaders of the Republican majority in the houses would go to the country with a much better chance of winning than the President could possibly count upon in the equivocal position into which

he had got himself. In July the houses passed, over the President's veto, a bill which continued the Freedmen's Bureau for two years; provided for the sale of public lands to the negroes on easy terms; appropriated the property of the confederate government to their education; and placed their civil rights under direct military protection. On the 18th of June the Committee on Reconstruction had made formal report of its views upon the situation. It was the policy of Congress enforced by reasons,—reasons which, it might be hoped, would fortify the minds of members of Congress and please the voters of the North in the coming contest. It declared that the governments of the States recently in secession were practically suspended, by reason both of the irregular character of the new governments which had been set up and of the reluctant acquiescence of the southern people in the results of the war; and that it was essential to the peace and sound policy of the Union that they should not be reinstated in their former privileges by Congress until they should have given substantial pledges, such pledges as Congress should demand, of their entire loyalty and submission. With that appeal the houses went to the country.

The friends of the President and of a moderate course in affairs, both Democrats and Republicans, came together in goodly numbers in convention, led by men whom the country knew and had reason to trust, and made a demonstration in favor of the policy which had been Mr. Lincoln's and which should be that of every man who loved peace and sought accommodation; and their action did not fail to make a considerable impression everywhere upon those who could put passion aside. But Mr. Johnson would not let quiet counsel alone. Incapable of prudence, scornful of soft words, a bitter hater, cast by nature for the rough contacts of personal conflict and debate, he spoke to the country himself. At mid-summer he made a journey to Chicago, and at almost every stopping place where the people crowded about his car he uttered, with that air of passion which always went with what he said, invectives against Congress so intemperate, so coarse, so hot with personal feeling that those who heard him looked upon him as almost a man distraught, thrown from his balance. He, not the leaders of Congress, seemed the radical, the apostle of passion; and his passion, men could say, was against the Union, not for it. He had set himself, his opponents declared, not to bring peace and restore the government to its integrity, but to perpetuate discord and cheat the party of the Union of its legitimate power.

Two days after Congress adjourned (July 30, 1866) a New Orleans mob broke up an irregular "constitutional convention" of negroes and their partisans with violence and bloodshed. In October the southern States, as if taking their cue from the President, not from Congress, began, one after the other, to reject the Fourteenth Amendment; and every impression that had been formed of reaction and recalcitrancy at the South was confirmed. The result of the elections was a foregone conclusion. A Republican majority was sent to the House as overwhelming as that which dominated the Congress about to expire; the Republican numbers in the Senate were maintained. The houses came together again in December heartened, resolute, triumphant, ready to override the President with a policy of Thorough which should put the fortunes of the South entirely at their disposal.

It was provided, by special Act, that the new Congress, just chosen, should convene, not in the following December, but on the 4th of March, 1867, in order that there might be no long vacation in which the President

THE RIOT IN NEW ORLEANS. SIEGE AND ASSAULT ON THE CONVENTION

would be left free to exercise his independent authority. Before the 4th of March came a Reconstruction Act had passed through the slow fires of debate and become law (March 2d) which embodied in their unmarred integrity the radical plans of the joint committee of fifteen. It provided that the States of the Confederacy, with the exception of Tennessee, which had already been permitted to adopt the Fourteenth Amendment and resume its place in Congress, should be grouped for purposes of government in five military districts, under the command of five general officers of the army to be appointed by the President. These military governors were to control and direct the processes of reconstruction. A temporary clause of the proposed Fourteenth Amendment, which the southern States had rejected, excluded from office, whether under the States or under the federal government, at the pleasure of Congress, all who had at any time or in any capacity, civil or military, taken oath to support the constitution of the United States and afterwards "engaged in insurrection or rebellion" against it, "or given aid or comfort to its enemies." The military governors under the Act were instructed to enroll in each State, under oath, only such citizens of voting age and of one year's residence within the State as they should deem qualified in accordance with the spirit of this prospective Amendment, the negroes, of course, included. They were to reject as voters all whom the proposed Amendment disqualified for office. They were then to order and hold in each State an election for delegates to a constitutional convention, in which none but the voters on their rolls should be allowed either to vote or to stand for election. They were to direct the conventions thus chosen to frame constitutions by which the elective suffrage should be extended without distinction to all classes of citizens included within the terms of the enrolment already made; and were to submit the constitutions thus framed to the same voters for ratification. When adopted by the voters, the constitutions which this plan of Thorough had brought into existence were to be sent to Congress, through the President, for final

approval. Each State, it was agreed, whose constitution Congress should approve was to be readmitted
to representation so soon as its legislature had ratified
the Fourteenth Amendment. Meanwhile, its government was to be deemed "provisional only, and in all
respects subject to the paramount authority of the United
States, at any time to abolish, control, or supersede

THE RIOT IN NEW ORLEANS. STRUGGLE FOR THE FLAG

it." The houses had already ordered, by resolution,
at their previous session, that the troops should be
kept at their stations in the South until Congress should
direct their recall. They now invested General Grant,
the General of the Army, with powers which made him,
and the army itself, practically independent of the
President. He was given sole authority to order the
removal or suspension of an officer, and military commanders were explicitly excused from accepting the

opinion of any civil official of the government in the construction of their powers.

Many motives had governed the members of Congress in the adoption of this extraordinary programme. Some had allowed themselves to be driven to radical courses by sheer bitter feeling against the President, who insisted so intemperately upon a course more simple, more moderate, more indulgent to the South; some could reason in statesmanlike fashion enough upon the premises of action, but could propose no alternative plan which seemed practicable or likely to command the support of the rank and file of their party; others were party men, without pretence or refinement of view, their whole temper hardened and embittered by the war and all its unpalatable consequences, and were willing to follow those who were frankly bent upon bringing the South to utter humiliation and penitent submission. Their leaders wished not only to give the negroes political privilege but also to put the white men of the South, for the nonce at any rate, under the negroes' heels. Every black voter, they cynically predicted, would once for all become under such tutelage a Republican voter, and the party which had conquered the South would rule it. Men who looked more scrupulously to their motives saw no way to withstand what they disapproved; were themselves convinced that something must be done to protect the helpless blacks; feared as much as the radicals themselves to see the real leaders of the South again in control; and, with misgivings not a few, lent their aid to the revolutionary programme.

The same months that saw the drastic Act debated and adopted witnessed a tragic revolution at the further south in which the government at Washington also

ARCHDUKE MAXIMILIAN

played its part. While the war for the Union was being fought, the emperor of France, looking to see that war rack the United States to pieces, had sent troops into Mexico and had set up a kingdom there for the Archduke Maximilian of Austria. He had got his opportunity in a way which had seemed for a time to make other great powers of Europe his partners and allies in the conquest. The closing days of the year 1857 had brought political upheaval and sharp civil war upon Mexico, which had resulted within two years in making Juarez, a Zapoteca Indian of singular capacity, master of the country. Juarez had not only confiscated the property of the church, but had also suspended by decree the payment of foreign debts, the debt of the Mexican nation itself included; and that decree had led, late in 1861, to a demonstration in force upon his coasts by the three nations, England, France, and Spain, who were Mexico's principal creditors. England and Spain would consent to do no more than was necessary to enforce the just claims of their citizens, and Napoleon had agreed to be governed by the terms of co-operation which they prescribed: the seizure, it might be, of a custom house or two, but no serious stroke against the sovereignty of the country. From the first, nevertheless, he had meant to disregard his engagements in the matter. He had long dreamed of conquest there in the south, and saw the time come now, as he thought, when he need fear no enforcement of the Monroe doctrine against him by the distracted government at the north. In despite of protests, he sent an army of conquest to Mexico, and, postponing open possession by France, put the Archduke Maximilian in the usurped place of authority, keeping his armies there to secure his throne and the predominance of France. The government at Washington protested but could do nothing more. The usurped throne stood, the armies of France remained, until

NAPOLEON III.

the war for the Union closed and the hands of the President were free. Then the protests from Washington took another tone and meaning, which Louis Napoleon was not self-deceived enough to suppose he could ignore.

41

American troops began to be massed in the neighborhood of the Mexican frontier, near the familiar ground of General Taylor's movements twenty years before; and the French government saw that it must yield. The French troops were withdrawn, and Maximilian was left to shape his fortunes alone. He was a man of high spirit, not apt to yield upon any point of honor, mindful of what he conceived to be his duty though he mistook it: a man of character, resolved to stand by his throne even though the French withdrew. The resolution cost him his life. Though he gathered a party about him, they were beaten by the partisans of Juarez. He was court-martialled, condemned, and shot. The melodramatic play which the histrionic genius of Napoleon had planned turned out a genuine tragedy, and a noble gentleman made a pitiful ending.

The same month that witnessed the withdrawal of the troops of France from Mexico saw final arrangements made for the withdrawal of Russia from the Pacific coast of North America. On the 30th of March, 1867, a treaty was agreed upon between Mr. Seward and the Russian minister at Washington for the sale of Alaska to the United States for the sum of seven million two hundred thousand dollars in gold. In May the treaty was ratified; and in the following October formal transfer of the great territory was effected. Mr. Monroe had checked the movement of Russian power southward upon the Pacific coast by his message of 1823, and in the forty odd years which had elapsed since that notable announcement of the supremacy of the United States in the western hemisphere the government at St. Petersburg had grown very indifferent to the retention of the bleak fragment of America

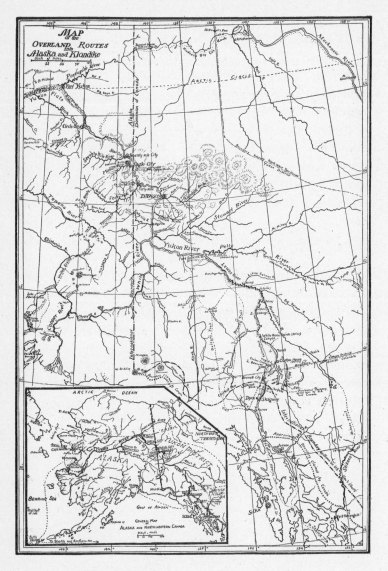

MAP OF ALASKA SHOWING THE GOLD-BEARING REGION

left in its hands,—so far away, so difficult, it might be, of defence. Informal communications in regard to its sale had passed between the two governments so long ago as 1859. Russia was anxious to sell; and the final purchase of 1867 was easily arranged for. There was a certain dramatic consistency in the association of the purchase of Alaska with the forced "withdrawal" of the French from Mexico. They stood together as logical consequences of the Monroe doctrine, whose avowed object had been to keep the American continents free from the control of European monarchies.

The deep effects wrought by Mr. Stevens's policy of Thorough in the southern States worked themselves out more slowly than the tragedy in Mexico, but with no less revolutionary force. Its operation brought on as profound a social upheaval as its most extreme advocates could have desired. The natural leaders of the South either would not take the oath prescribed or were excluded from the right to enroll themselves as voters by the very terms of the Reconstruction Act. The negroes were the chief voters. The conventions which they chose and the governments which those conventions set up were constituted to secure them power. In Virginia, Mississippi, and Texas, after the conventions had acted, the white voters rallied strong enough at the polls, as it turned out, to defeat the constitutions they had framed when they were submitted for ratification; but they were only kept so much the longer under military government, and were obliged to accept them at last. In Georgia the new constitution was adopted; but the statutes of the reconstituted State debarred negroes from holding office, and Congress

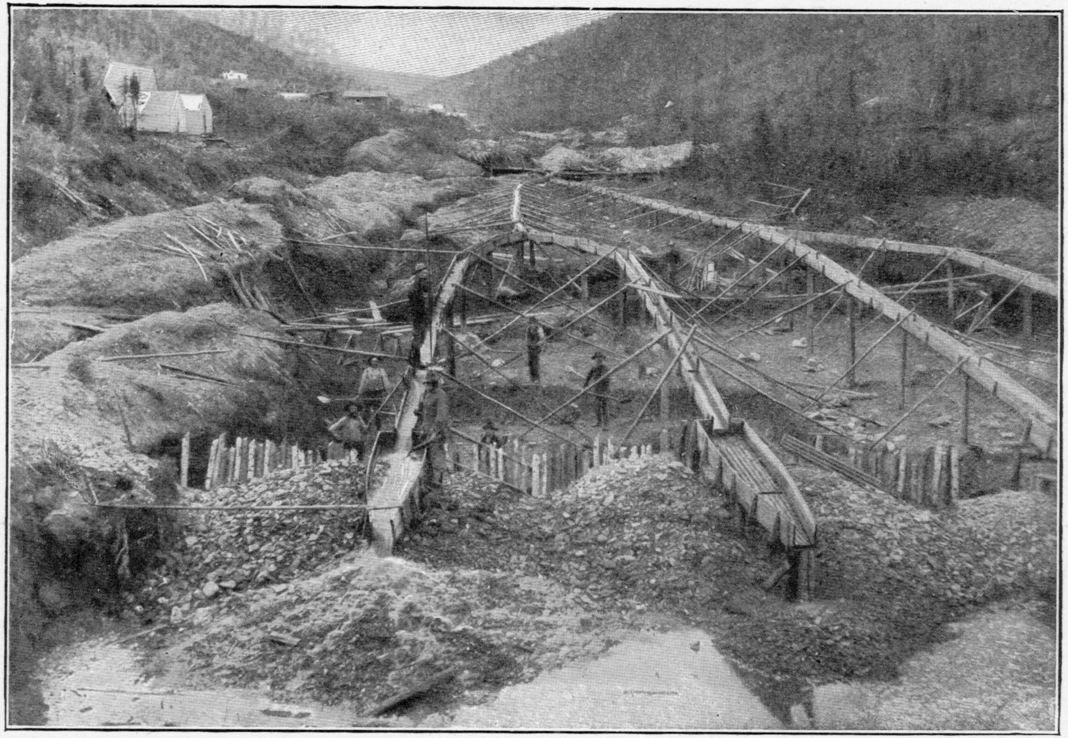

SLUICE-WASHING FOR GOLD IN THE KLONDIKE

would not admit her to representation so long as those statutes stood unrepealed. In the Carolinas, in Florida, in Alabama, Arkansas, and Louisiana nothing stayed the execution of the congressional plan, and by mid-summer, 1868, Congress was ready to readmit those States to representation. But South Carolina, Louisiana, and Florida were utterly given over in the process to the government of adventurers.

Negroes constituted the majority of their electorates; but political power gave them no advantage of their own. Adventurers swarmed out of the North to cozen, beguile, and use them. These men, mere "carpet baggers" for the most part, who brought nothing with them, and had nothing to bring, but a change of clothing and their wits, became the new masters of the blacks. They gained the confidence of the negroes, obtained for themselves the more lucrative offices, and lived upon the public treasury, public contracts, and their easy control of affairs. For the negroes there was nothing but occasional allotments of abandoned or forfeited land, the pay of petty offices, a *per diem* allowance as members of the conventions and the state legislatures which their new masters made business for, or the wages of servants in the various offices of administration. Their ignorance and credulity made them easy dupes. A petty favor, a slender stipend, a trifling perquisite, a bit of poor land, a piece of money satisfied or silenced them. It was enough, for the rest, to play upon their passions. They were easily taught to hate the men who had once held them in slavery, and to follow blindly the political party which had brought on the war of their emancipation.

There were soon lands enough and to spare out of

46

which to make small gifts to them without sacrifice of gain on the part of their new masters. In Mississippi, before the work of the carpet baggers was done, six hundred and forty thousand acres of land had been forfeited for taxes, twenty *per cent.* of the total acreage of the State. The state tax levy for 1871 was four times as great as the levy for 1869 had been; that for 1873 eight times as great; that for 1874 fourteen times. The impoverished planters could not carry the intolerable burden of taxes, and gave their lands up to be sold by the sheriff. There were few who could buy. The lands lay waste and neglected or were parcelled out at nominal rates among the negroes. In South Carolina the taxes of 1871 aggregated $2,000,000 as against a total of $400,000 in 1860, though the taxable values of the State were but $184,000,000 in 1871 and had been $490,000,000 in 1860. There were soon lands to be had for the asking wherever the tax gatherer of the new governments had pressed his claims. The assessed valuation of property in the city of New Orleans sank, during the eight years of carpet-bag rule, from $146,718,790 to $88,613,930. Four years and a half of "reconstruction" cost Louisiana $106,020,337. The demoralization of affairs in Louisiana had begun in 1862, when General Butler took possession of the city of New Orleans. The rich spoils of the place had proved too much for the principles of the men intrusted with the management of her affairs in times when law was silent; and the political adventurers who came out of the North to take charge of the new government set up under Mr. Stevens's plan of reconstruction found the work they had come to do already begun.

Taxes, of course, did not suffice. Enormous debts

were piled up to satisfy the adventurers. The cases of Louisiana and South Carolina were no doubt the worst, but other States suffered in proportion to the opportunities they afforded for safe depredation. In 1868 the debt of South Carolina had been $5,000,000; in 1872 it was nearly $30,000,000. The debt of Louisiana

BENJAMIN FRANKLIN BUTLER

in 1868 had been between six and seven millions; in 1872 it was $50,000,000. Where the new rulers acted with less assurance and immunity or with smaller resources at hand, debts grew more slowly, but the methods of spoliation were everywhere much the same; and with the rise of debts went always the disappearance of all assets wherewith to pay them. Treasuries were swept clean. Immense grants were made in aid of public works which were never completed, sometimes not even begun. Railways were subsidized, and the subsidies, by one device or another, converted into outright gifts, which went into the pockets of those who had procured them, not into the building or equipment of the road. A vast burden of debt was piled up for coming generations to carry; the present generation was much too poor to pay anything.

The real figures of the ruin wrought no man could get at. It was not to be expressed in state taxes or state debts. The increase in the expenditure and indebtedness of counties and towns, of school districts and cities, represented an aggregate greater even than that of the ruinous sums which had drained the treasuries and mortgaged the resources of the governments of the States; and men saw with their own eyes what was going on at their own doors. What was afoot at the capitals of their States they only read of in the newspapers or heard retailed in the gossip of the street, but the affairs of their own villages and country-sides they saw corrupted, mismanaged, made base use of under their very eyes. There the negroes themselves were the office holders, men who could not so much as write their names and who knew none of the uses of authority except its insolence. It was there that the policy of the congressional leaders wrought its perfect work of fear, demoralization, disgust, and social revolution.

No one who thought justly or tolerantly could think that this veritable overthrow of civilization in the South had been foreseen or desired by the men who had followed Mr. Stevens and Mr. Wade and Mr. Morton in

their policy of rule or ruin. That handful of leaders it
was, however, hard to acquit of the charge of knowing
and intending the ruinous consequences of what they
had planned. They would take counsel of moderation
neither from northern men nor from southern. They
were proof against both fact and reason in their determination to "put the white South under the heel of
the black South." They did not know the region with
which they were dealing. Northern men who did know
it tried to inform them of its character and of the danger
and folly of what they were undertaking; but they refused to be informed, did not care to know, were in any
case fixed upon the accomplishment of a single object.
Their colleagues, their followers, kept, many of them,
a cooler mind, a more prudent way of thought, but
could not withstand them. They, too, were ignorant
of the South. They saw but a little way into the future,
had no means of calculating what the effects of these
drastic measures would be upon the life and action of
the South, and lacked even the knowledge of mere
human nature which might have served them instead
of an acquaintance with the actual men they were dealing with. They had not foreseen that to give the suffrage to the negroes and withhold it from the more
capable white men would bestow political power, not
upon the negroes, but upon white adventurers, as much
the enemies of the one race as of the other. In that
day of passion, indeed, they had not stopped to speculate
what the effects would be. Their object had been to
give the negro political power in order that he might
defend his own rights, as voters everywhere else might
defend theirs. They had not recked of consequences;
for a little while they had not cared what they might be.

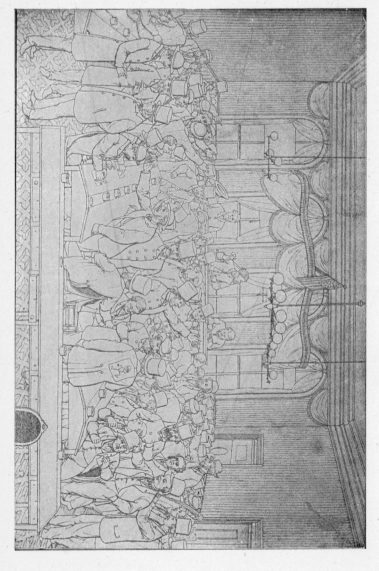

AN EXCITING DAY IN THE BOARD OF BROKERS, "ON THE RISE," NEW YORK CITY, 1862

They had prepared the way for the ruin of the South, but they had hardly planned to ruin it.

News of what was going on in the South was not slow to make its way to the ears of the country at large; but the editors of northern newspapers at first refused to credit what they heard. Men dismissed the reports with an easy laugh, as simply the South's cry of exasperation that the negro should have been given the ballot and the power to rule. But incredulity grew more and more difficult; the accounts of what was going on grew more and more circumstantial; proof came close upon the heels of rumor; and opinion began to veer unsteadily. It shifted not only because of the disquieting news that came from the South, but also because of the desperate strain the government itself was put to at Washington by reason of the open breach and warfare between the President and Congress. The masterful men who led the congressional majority had not contented themselves with putting such laws as they chose upon the statute books despite the President's vetoes; they had gone much further and taken steps to make the President a mere figurehead even in administration, and put themselves in virtual control of the executive *personnel* of the government. Along with the Reconstruction Act of 1867, which placed the governments of the southern States in their hands, they had forced through, over the President's veto, a Tenure of Office Act which deprived the President of the power of removal from office except by the advice and with the consent of the Senate. It gave even to cabinet officers a fixed tenure of four years. They could be dismissed within the four years of the presidential term only by the consent of the Senate.

Here was a deliberate reversal of the constitutional practice of more than two generations. The debates of the first Congress under the constitution, the views of the statesmen who had framed the law of the government, the opinions of lawyers, the unbroken practice of sixteen presidents had been thought to establish beyond question the right of the chief magistrate to remove federal administrative officials at his pleasure. Congress, it seemed, was ready to override law and precedent alike to make good its mastery.

Mr. Johnson was not the man to decline such a challenge. After fighting the policy of Congress in matters purely legislative with caustic vetoes and bitter condemnation he was not likely to submit to have his very powers of administration stripped away without resistance carried to the utmost bounds. He had kept Mr. Lincoln's cabinet; but he had not relished the attitude of one or two of its members towards him. It had been hard enough for Mr. Lincoln, even, with his shrewd and kindly insight into the real nature of the man and his love for the sheer force and audacity with which he administered his critical office in days almost of revolution, to endure the wilful arrogance of Edwin M. Stanton, the Secretary of War; it was quite impossible for Mr. Johnson to endure it. It was something more than wilfulness that Mr. Stanton showed in his relations with Mr. Johnson. He became openly a partisan of the radical leaders in Congress, and set himself to defeat the President at his own council table. He administered the affairs of his Department as if he considered it an independent branch of the government; carried out the instructions of the President with regard to the South in a way to discredit as much as possible the policy which they embodied; and seemed bent upon maintaining the Department of War as a sort of counterpoise to the presidency itself until a man acceptable to the Republican majority in the houses should come to the head of the government. Mr. Johnson had wished from the first to be rid of him, but had wished also to preserve unbroken the tradition of policy handed on to him from Mr. Lincoln, and had hesitated to ask for his resignation. He determined now to make Mr. Stanton's case a case for the test of his prerogative and of the Tenure of Office Act which sought to curtail it. In August (1867), during the congressional recess, he demanded Mr. Stanton's resignation. Mr. Stanton refused to resign, and the President suspended him from office, as the terms of the Act itself permitted, putting General Grant in his place. When Congress reassembled in December the Senate refused to sanction the removal, and Mr. Stanton resumed his office. The President once again issued an order for his removal, and Mr. Stanton again refused to quit his office, appealing to the House for protection. On February 24, 1868, the House voted to impeach the President for high crimes and misdemeanors.

His only offences were that he had added to his vetoes unmeasured abuse of the houses and their leaders and that he had disregarded an Act of Congress in his removal of Mr. Stanton; but the impeachment had been resolved upon as a political, not as a judicial, process of removal, in passion, not in cool judgment,—in the spirit of the men who in Mr. Jefferson's day had sought to make it a means of party mastery against the judges of the federal courts. From the 5th of March to the 16th of May the unedifying trial dragged on. Even while it pended the President went incorrigibly up and down the country speaking with his accustomed unguarded passion and open defiance of every one concerned against him in the long series of controversies which had brought the trial on. Fortunately there were men among the Republicans of the Senate who put their consciences as lawyers and their scruples as statesmen before their allegiance to their party leaders. On the 16th of May the impeachment broke down. The first test vote was taken; seven Republican senators voted with the ten Democrats of the upper house against the thirty-five Republican senators who cast their votes for conviction. The managers had failed to secure the two-thirds necessary to convict; and a verdict of acquittal was entered. The Secretary of War resigned his office, and the contest was over.

It was, it turned out, the President's noisy, unapplauded exit from public trust and employment. Four days after the failure of the impeachment proceedings the Republican nominating convention met at Chicago which was to name a candidate for the presidential term to begin on the 4th of March, 1869. It nominated General Grant, unanimously and with genuine enthusiasm, because he was a faithful officer and no politician. Mr. Johnson had shown himself a Democrat, not a Republican, as party lines had been drawn upon the issue of reconstruction; but the Democrats wanted him for another term as little as the Republicans did. Their convention nominated Mr. Horatio Seymour, of New York, a man of high character and unimpeachable reputation in affairs, and went to the country on the question of reconstruction. The result no one seriously doubted from the first. Few voters in the Republican

ranks at the North had as yet suffered themselves to
see anything in Mr. Stevens's plan of Thorough to
daunt either their taste or their principles; the votes

HORATIO SEYMOUR

of most of the southern States then reconstructed were
turned over to the Republican candidate, as expected,
by the negro voters; and Mr. Seymour obtained but
eighty ballots in the electoral college to General Grant's
two hundred and fourteen. It was a significant thing,

nevertheless, that in a total popular vote of more than 5,700,000 General Grant's majority was but a little more than three hundred thousand. Mr. Seymour had carried New York and New Jersey at the centre of the old Union. A slight shifting of the winds of opinion might bring weather on which the policy of reconstruction devised in Congress could not survive. But a more normal season seemed at hand. The country was to have at least peace at its capital, a President trusted by the leaders of Congress. Mr. Johnson's tempestuous and troubled term was over, and a plain soldier again at the head of the government.

Congress did not wait for General Grant's inauguration, however, to go forward with its policy of reconstruction. Before the end of February, 1869 (February 25th), it proposed to the States a Fifteenth Amendment intended to lay in the constitution itself the foundations of negro suffrage which had as yet only the support of the Reconstruction Acts of 1867, mere statutes. "The right of citizens of the United States to vote," so ran its terms, "shall not be denied or abridged by the United States or any State on account of race, color, or previous condition of servitude." New Jersey, Delaware, Maryland, Kentucky, California, and Oregon rejected it; Tennessee did not act upon it; but thirty of the thirty-seven States accepted it, and it became part of the constitution. Virginia, Georgia, Mississippi, and Texas had not yet been reconstructed to the satisfaction of Congress; the acceptance of this new Amendment, accordingly, the enactment in perpetuity of the principle of the Reconstruction Act, was made a condition precedent to their readmission to Congress, as the acceptance of the Thirteenth Amendment, which

57

gave the negroes their freedom, and of the Fourteenth, which made them citizens of the United States and of the States of their residence, had been. This, too, was to be part of the hard-driven bargain of reconstruction before the Republican leaders would be satisfied. The dominance of the negroes in the South was to be made a principle of the very constitution of the Union. A long year went by before three fourths of the States had ratified the radical Amendment, but the necessary votes came in at last, and on the 30th of March, 1870, the new article was officially declared in force.

The price of the policy to which it gave the final touch of permanence was the temporary disintegration of southern society and the utter, apparently the irretrievable, alienation of the South from the political party whose mastery it had been Mr. Stevens's chief aim to perpetuate. The white men of the South were aroused by the mere instinct of self-preservation to rid themselves, by fair means or foul, of the intolerable burden of governments sustained by the votes of ignorant negroes and conducted in the interest of adventurers: governments whose incredible debts were incurred that thieves might be enriched, whose increasing loans and taxes went to no public use but into the pockets of party managers and corrupt contractors. There was no place of open action or of constitutional agitation, under the terms of reconstruction, for the men who were the real leaders of the southern communities. Its restrictions shut white men of the older order out from the suffrage even. They could act only by private combination, by private means, as a force outside the government, hostile to it, proscribed by it, of whom opposition and bitter resistance was expected, and expected

with defiance. Sober men kept their heads; prudent
men saw how sad an increase of passion would come
out of hasty counsels of strife, an open grapple between
those outlawed and those appointed to govern. Men
whom experience had chastened saw that only the
slow processes of opinion could mend the unutterable
errors of a time like that. But there were men to whom
counsels of prudence seemed as ineffectual as they
were unpalatable, men who could not sit still and suffer
what was now put upon them. It was folly for them
to give rein to their impulses; it was impossible for
them to do nothing.

They took the law into their own hands, and began
to attempt by intimidation what they were not allowed
to attempt by the ballot or by any ordered course of
public action. They began to do by secret concert and
association what they could not do in avowed parties.
Almost by accident a way was found to succeed which
led insensibly farther and farther afield into the ways
of violence and outlawry. In May, 1866, a little group
of young men in the Tennessee village of Pulaski, finding time hang heavy on their hands after the excitements of the field, so lately abandoned, formed a secret
club for the mere pleasure of association, for private
amusement,—for anything that might promise to break
the monotony of the too quiet place, as their wits might
work upon the matter, and one of their number suggested that they call themselves the *Kuklos*, the Circle.
Secrecy and mystery were at the heart of the pranks
they planned: secrecy with regard to the membership
of their Circle, secrecy with regard to the place and
the objects of its meetings; and the mystery of disguise
and of silent parade when the comrades rode abroad

at night when the moon was up: a white mask, a tall
cardboard hat, the figures of man and horse sheeted
like a ghost, and the horses' feet muffled to move without sound of their approach. It was the delightful
discovery of the thrill of awesome fear, the woeful looking for of calamity that swept through the country-
sides as they moved from place to place upon their silent
visitations, coming no man could say whence, going
upon no man knew what errand, that put thought of
mischief into the minds of the frolicking comrades. It
threw the negroes into a very ecstasy of panic to see
these sheeted "Ku Klux" move near them in the
shrouded night; and their comic fear stimulated the
lads who excited it to many an extravagant prank and
mummery. No one knew or could discover who the
masked players were; no one could say whether they
meant serious or only innocent mischief; and the zest
of the business lay in keeping the secret close.

Here was a very tempting and dangerous instrument
of power for days of disorder and social upheaval, when
law seemed set aside by the very government itself,
and outsiders, adventurers, were in the seats of authority,
the poor negroes, and white men without honor, their
only partisans. Year by year the organization spread,
from county to county, from State to State. Every
country-side wished to have its own Ku Klux, founded
in secrecy and mystery like the mother "Den" at Pulaski,
until at last there had sprung into existence a great
Ku Klux Klan, an "Invisible Empire of the South,"
bound together in loose organization to protect the
southern country from some of the ugliest hazards of a
time of revolution. The objects of the mysterious
brotherhood grew serious fast enough. It passed from

jest to earnest. Men took hold of it who rejoiced to find in it a new instrument of political power: men half outlawed, denied the suffrage, without hope of justice

TWO MEMBERS OF THE KU KLUX KLAN

in the courts, who meant to take this means to make their will felt. "They were to protect their people from indignities and wrongs; to succor the suffering, particularly the families of dead confederate soldiers"; to enforce what they conceived to be the real laws of their States "and defend the constitution of the United States and all laws passed in conformity thereto; to aid in executing all constitutional laws and protect the people from unlawful seizures and from trial otherwise than by jury." Similar secret orders grew up alongside the great Klan, or in States where its "dens" had not been established: Knights of the White Camellia, Pale Faces, Constitutional Union Guards, the White Brotherhood, to serve the same ends by the same means. The Knights of the White Camellia, founded in New Orleans in the winter of 1867–1868, spread their organization abroad more widely even than the Ku Klux Klan.

It was impossible to keep such a power in hand. Sober men governed the counsels and moderated the plans of these roving knights errant; but it was lawless work at best. They had set themselves, after the first year or two of mere mischievous frolic had passed, to right a disordered society through the power of fear. Men of hot passions who could not always be restrained carried their plans into effect. Reckless men not of their order, malicious fellows of the baser sort who did not feel the compulsions of honor and who had private grudges to satisfy, imitated their disguises and borrowed their methods. What was done passed beyond mere mummery, mere visiting the glimpses of the moon and making night hideous, that they might cause mere "fools of nature horridly to shake their disposition with thoughts beyond the reaches of their souls." It became the chief object of the night-riding comrades to silence or drive from the country the principal mischief-makers of the reconstruction régime, whether white or black. The negroes were generally easy enough to deal with: a thorough fright usually disposed them to make utter submission, resign their parts in affairs, leave the country,—do anything their ghostly visitors demanded. But white men were less tractable; and here and there even a negro ignored or defied them. The regulators would not always threaten and never execute their threats. They backed their commands, when need arose, with violence. Houses were surrounded in the night and burned, and the inmates shot as they fled, as in the dreadful days of border warfare. Men were dragged from their houses and tarred and feathered. Some who defied the vigilant visitors came mysteriously to some sudden death.

The more ardent regulators made no nice discriminations. All northern white men or women who came into the South to work among the negroes, though they were but school teachers, were in danger of their enmity and silent onset. Many of the teachers who worked among the negroes did in fact do mischief as deep as any political adventurer. The lessons taught in their schools seemed to be lessons of self-assertion against the whites: they seemed too often to train their pupils to be aggressive Republican politicians and mischief-makers between the races. The innocent and enlightened among them suffered in the general opinion from the errors of those who deliberately sowed discord; and the regulators too often failed to discriminate between those who made trouble and those who fulfilled their gentle errand in peace and good temper.

The ranks of those who flocked into the South to take part in the reconstruction of the States and the habilitation of the negro for his life of freedom were strangely mixed of good and bad. The teachers came

63

upon an errand of mercy and humanity, but came too many of them with bitter thoughts and intolerant purpose against the white people of the South, upon whom, as they did not reflect, the fortunes of the negro in any case depended. The politicians came for the most part like a predatory horde; but here and there emerged a man of integrity, of principle, of wise and moderate counsel, who in the long run won the confidence even of those who hated with an ineradicable hatred the party and the practice of federal control which he represented. The Ku Klux and those who masqueraded in their guise struck at first only at those who made palpable mischief between the races or set just law aside to make themselves masters; but their work grew under their hands, and their zest for it. Brutal crimes were committed; the innocent suffered with the guilty; a reign of terror was brought on, and society was infinitely more disturbed than defended. Law seemed oftentimes given over. The right to the writ of *habeas corpus* was again and again suspended to check the lawless work. At least one governor of the reconstruction period sent to his adjutant general lists of leading citizens proscribed, with the suggestion that those whose names were specially marked should be tried by court martial and executed at once before the use of the writ should be restored. One lawless force seemed in contest with another.

Such was the disturbing subject matter of the news which crept north during the first year of General Grant's administration as President. It found business as well as politics moved by its own uneasy excitements. The year 1869 witnessed an attempt on the part of a small group of brokers to corner the gold market, singularly audacious, singularly fatal in its consequences to the business of the country. Their operations culminated on a certain "Black Friday," the 24th of September, 1869. All foreign trade balances, all pay-

SCENE IN THE GOLD ROOM, NEW YORK CITY, ON "BLACK FRIDAY"

ments of customs duties at the ports, required gold, and the Wall Street firm of Smith, Gould, Martin & Co., in association with a few others, undertook nothing less than to get control of all the gold in the country that was available for such purposes, outside the Treasury of the United States. They sought to keep the gold in the Treasury out of their way in the market by interesting friends of the President to ply him with arguments based upon public policy to which they thought he would be amenable, and hurried their operations to a crisis while the arguments told; bought gold on every hand, at any figures; and forced its price up, up, until the end came on that Friday which the Street was never to forget. On that day they had the prices and the stock of gold almost at their disposal when the news came that the President had ordered the sub-treasury of the United States at New York to sell gold from the vaults of the government for the relief of the market and it was known that the hundred million which the government held had begun to be released. Then the crash came, and the ruin the operators had wrought, for themselves and others, was laid bare. Trade at home as well as abroad depended upon the available stores of gold. That desperate speculation had upset credit. The movement of the crops halted; foreign trade came to a standstill; the West would not deal with the East; the East could not deal over sea. No man who handled money knew just where he stood. The business of the continent was racked to its centre; and every man who knew the money market knew that it would be many a weary month, it might be many a weary year, before the demoralizing effects of that day would pass away. The operators who had brought the panic on shielded themselves in the courts, and even the immediate ruin they had wrought upon their victims could not be repaired.

There were abundant crops, and business lacked nothing to make it prosperous but a steady money market. The census taken in 1870 showed the population of the country increased by more than seven millions since 1860, for all it had been a decade filled with death and war. Even the South had added some eight hundred thousand to her reckoning. Industry went forward at a quiet pace, and the wealth of the country grew in the very season of financial panic. It was the unquiet spirit of adventure that upset affairs. The war had thrown business from its ordinary courses. The huge purchases of the War Department, the unusual peril of the seas so long as the confederate privateers were abroad, the necessary hazards of business while war filled every transaction with conjecture had bred the speculative temper and quickened the instinct for adventurous operations on the grand scale; had made men apt at managing "corners" and reckless what risks they added to the legitimate hazards of trade.

Embarrassments alike of business and of feeling, created by the war and all that had come in its train, cleared very slowly away. Local storm though it was, the war had not failed to send its airs abroad and create international disturbances as well as domestic. It had particularly threatened to bring about serious misunderstandings between England and the United States. Most of the confederate privateers and swift cruisers that had played havoc with the sea-going trade of the United States during the earlier years of the war had been built in English ship yards and had come from English ports. Their arms and equipment had been bought in England. Their officers had waited for them in England, drawing their pay, the while, through English banks. The English government acknowledged itself bound to prevent all overt attempts of its subjects to aid or arm the enemies of a nation with which it was at peace, and to prevent the use of its ports and waters as a base of naval operations against

Charles Francis Adams   CHARLES FRANCIS ADAMS

her; but it did not consider itself bound, as the government of the United States contended that it should, to canvass every case of suspicion in such matters and detain vessels merely upon reasonable ground of belief that they were intended for uses inconsistent with its neutrality. Mr. Charles Francis Adams, the minister of the United States, had brought every case promptly to the attention of her Majesty's ministers and in more than one case had laid convincing evidence before them of the character and destination of vessels being fitted out in English ship yards for the service of the Confederacy; and the government at Washington could not but connect their slow and indifferent action in the cases submitted, their apparent unwillingness to examine the evidence, their slackness in taking steps to seize the suspected vessels with their manifest friendliness, or at least benevolent neutrality, towards the Confederate States, their recognition of their belligerent rights, their half inclination to accord them full recognition as an independent power. It soon became evident that entire cordiality of feeling between the two governments could not be restored until the matter had been brought to a definite reckoning and final adjustment.

The reckoning came at the very outset of General Grant's administration. Mr. Seward had tried to bring it about while Mr. Johnson was President, but the Senate had rejected the method of settlement he had been willing to adopt, and an arrangement agreeable to both governments was not arrived at until the spring of 1871. In May of that year, a Joint High Commission appointed by the President and the ministers in London and sitting in Washington, agreed upon a treaty, acceptable to the Senate, which referred the claims of the United States against Great Britain on account of the damage inflicted by the *Alabama*, the

Florida, the *Shenandoah,* and all other confederate
vessels alleged to have been fitted out in British ports,
"generically known as the Alabama claims," to the
arbitration of a tribunal of five persons to be named
by the President of the United States, the Queen of England, the King of Italy, the President of the Swiss Confederation, and the Emperor of Brazil respectively, and

THE BURNING OF THE JACOB BELL BY THE ALABAMA

to sit at Geneva, in Switzerland. The treaty of Washington,—so it was called,—provided also for the settlement of other matters in dispute between the two governments which touched their permanent interests: the
right of American fishermen to catch fish upon the
Canadian coasts and of Canadian fishermen to make
their catches upon the northern coasts of the United
States, and the exact line of boundary between the
United States and British North America within the
streams which separated them and within the channel

HÔTEL BEAU-RIVAGE, GENEVA, HEADQUARTERS OF THE AMERICAN ARBITRATORS

between Vancouver's Island and the continent; but the Alabama claims for the moment seemed to all eyes to stand at the front of the matter. On the 14th of September, 1872, after a three months' hearing, the Geneva tribunal rendered a decision in favor of the United States, only the English member of the court dissenting. It awarded to the United States $15,500,000 in damages. But the strain of the matter had been taken off by the treaty; the decision of the tribunal ended, not a controversy, but a judicial process at the end of controversy.

The strain of domestic politics was enough to withdraw heat from such matters when once they had become mere matters of business. The reconstruction even of those southern States in which the establishment of negro majorities had miscarried and the white voters had mustered strong and stubborn enough to reject the laws Congress tried to thrust upon them (Virginia, Georgia, Mississippi, and Texas) was complete by midsummer, 1870. But the mere completion of the formal process of reconstruction, as planned in Congress, did not mean order or the quiet settlement of affairs in the South. The white men, with whom effective initiative and the real weight of predominance rested in any case, had had their wits quickened and their temper hardened by what the Republican leaders had done. They were shut out from the use of the ballot and from every open and legitimate part in affairs, but they had come at their power in another way. Those who loved mastery and adventure directed the work of the Ku Klux. Those whose tastes and principles made such means unpalatable brought their influence to bear along every line of counsel or of management that

promised to thrust the carpet bagger out of office and discourage the negro in the use of his vote. Congress saw where they meant to regain their mastery, at the polls, and by what means, the intimidation and control of the negroes without regard to law,—the law thrust upon them, not their own; and hastened to set up a new barrier of statute against them.

In May, 1870, it had passed an Act which put southern elections and the registration of voters in the southern States under the superintendence and virtual control of federal supervisors and marshals, who were empowered to protect all voters in the exercise of their right of suffrage, and whose complaints were to be heard, not by the courts of the States, but by the circuit courts of the United States alone. At its next session it still further strengthened the Act. The forty-second Congress met on the 4th of March, 1871, in extraordinary session, to continue legislation to the same end. Not merely the acts of registration and voting needed to be guarded; every privilege conferred upon the negro as an incident of his new freedom seemed in need of protection: the Republican leaders were determined that the Fourteenth as well as the Fifteenth Amendment should be buttressed about by penal legislation and the whole force of the government, if necessary, brought to bear to put them into effectual execution. A committee of seven senators and fourteen representatives was appointed to inquire into the actual condition of the South and ascertain the facts with regard to the alleged outrages there, and a drastic Act was passed (April 20, 1871) which was meant to crush the Ku Klux Klan and all lawless bands acting after its fashion. Its provisions made such acts, whether of violence or of mere intimidation, as the secret societies of the South had committed conspiracy against the government of the United States, punishable by heavy fines or by imprisonment, or by both fine and imprisonment, and authorized the President, whenever the state authorities were unable or unwilling to prevent or check them, to use the land and naval forces of the federal government for their suppression, as against an insurrection. It authorized him, also, until the close of the next regular session of Congress, to suspend at his pleasure the writ of *habeas corpus* "during the continuance of such rebellion against the United States," in such portions of the southern country as seemed to him most touched by the disorders of the time or most under the control of the secret associations. The Act gave to the federal courts which were empowered to enforce it the right to exclude from their juries persons suspected of sympathizing with those who violated its provisions. It was meant to destroy root and branch the organizations which had set themselves to annul the rights of the negroes. The Act of May, 1870, had made it a criminal offence "to go in disguise upon the highway, or upon the premises of another" by way of conspiracy "to deprive any citizen of his constitutional rights," striking directly at the secret orders and their more lawless imitators.

General Grant used the powers conferred upon him with the energy and directness of a soldier, as Congress had expected. On the 12th of October, 1871, singling out nine counties of South Carolina in which such acts as Congress had aimed its blow at were most frequent, he called upon the members of all illegal associations within them to surrender their arms and disguises within five days. Five days afterwards, his proclamation not having been heeded, he suspended the privilege of the writ of *habeas corpus* in the counties named, and two hundred arrests, followed promptly enough by prosecution and conviction, were immediately made. It was easy, with the powers bestowed by the Act upon the federal judges, to push trials to a quick consummation, and to eliminate all reasonable chance of escaping conviction. And the action of the President in South Carolina was but a beginning of his action throughout the South. Everywhere that the secret orders or the reckless fellows who plied their means of intimidation without scruple or principle or public object had been most active arrests and prosecutions came thick and fast; and within but a little more than a year an end was made of the business.

But, though the Act had worked its drastic remedy, peace, accommodation, the rational relationships between race and race upon which alone a reasonable order of life could rest, were, it might be, further off than ever. The joint committee of Senate and House which Congress had appointed to accompany the execution of the Act with a thorough-going inquiry into the actual condition of the South filled thirteen volumes with the reports of their investigations. They found no justification for what the white men of the South, desperate to free themselves from the rule of negroes and adventurers, had done; they drew forth from their witnesses little but what was dark and of evil omen; they made no serious attempt to understand the causes which underlay conspiracy and chronic disorder; they only laid before the country a mass of undigested testimony, crude, unverifiable, and uttered their expected

76

condemnation of a people at bay. But the country began to see for itself the real philosophy of the painful story. Significant rifts began to show themselves

R. Toombs   ROBERT TOOMBS

in opinion. It began to be plainly evident to all who were willing to look facts in the face what Mr. Stevens and his radical colleagues had really accomplished by their policy of Thorough. They had made the

white men of the South implacable enemies, not of the
Union, but of the party that had saved the Union and
which now carried its affairs in its hands. Their reconstruction, whose object had been, not the rehabilitation of the southern governments, but the political enfranchisement of the negroes, had wrought a work of
bitterness incomparably deeper, incomparably more
difficult to undo, than the mere effects of war and a
virtual conquest of arms. They had made the ascendency of the party of the Union seem to the men of the
South nothing less than the corruption and destruction
of their society, a reign of ignorance, a régime of power
basely used; and this revolt, these secret orders with
their ugly work of violence and terror, these infinite,
desperate shifts to be rid of the burden and night-
mare of what had been put upon them, were the consequence.

The reactions of opinion were slow. The country,
though it grew uneasy, was not yet ready to put itself
in the hands of the Democratic party, which had opposed the war, and which still suffered in the thought
of the voters the discredit of its old alliance with the
slave owners. The presidential election of 1872 came
and went without disturbing the supremacy of the
majority. But it brought to light many things that
gravely disquieted the Republican leaders. Thoughtful and influential men whose support they could ill
afford to lose, were, they perceived, being alienated
from them. It was a serious matter that their plans
in the South had so miscarried and required even yet
the policing of whole districts by armed men. Evidently
nothing but force sustained them, or could sustain
them; and no humane or thoughtful man could look

with complaisance upon a perpetual subjection of the South to federal arms. The administration of southern affairs from Washington wore, moreover, from another angle an unhandsome appearance. Its objects seemed to be, not so much the enforcement of constitutional rights as the aggrandizement of personal adherents of the President and of the close partisans of the Republican leaders who were most in his confidence. The troublesome, unwholesome matter of official patronage played too prominent a part in the motives of the government, and made the treatment of southern affairs seem only a phase of the general "spoils system" of appointment to office which seemed to have fastened itself upon the party organization of the country.

It was bad enough that the federal offices should be emptied wholesale upon a change of parties in the administration, to make room for the partisans of the successful leaders, as they had been when Mr. Lincoln came to the presidency,—as they had been at every change of parties since General Jackson's day; but that had at least given political solidarity to the administration and made the President in some sort master in the counsels of his party. Now a new and sinister sign was added that the official patronage of the government was to be used, not to strengthen and solidify the administration, but to give secure political power to local managers who were to be permitted to dictate to the President whom he should appoint to office. In one State after another there emerged some one man, —a senator, a representative, a federal official of high office,—who was recognized as the President's only adviser with regard to all appointments within his State; and all federal office holders within that State

became by natural consequence his sycophants. In
the South these petty masters were too often the political
adventurers who had been drawn to their places of
preferment by the temptations of the process of reconstruction, when the negroes waited to be used, or men
who were themselves the subservient tools of politicians
in Washington. General Grant himself felt the demoralization of the system very keenly and desired its
radical reformation, but was easily imposed upon by
men whom he trusted, and trusted men without discrimination. He had great simplicity of character.
He judged men shrewdly enough when he saw them
in action, but had little insight into their real motives
and character when associated with them in counsel.
It seemed to him unnatural, unfaithful, as it had seemed
to General Jackson, to doubt or distrust his friends,
—not so much because he was a soldier and ready to
stand by his comrades with stout allegiance as because,
like most men of simple nature, he deemed others as
honest as himself, and suspicion a thing for rogues to
harbor.

The President had alienated, moreover, certain men
whose support he could not afford to dispense with.
He had set his heart upon the annexation of Santo
Domingo to the United States, and had come to an
open breach with Mr. Charles Sumner, chairman of
the Senate Committee on Foreign Affairs upon the
matter. That and many other things, great and small,
had driven Mr. Horace Greeley also into opposition,
the erratic, trenchant editor of the New York *Tribune*.
Mr. Sumner seemed to a great many men in the country
to stand for the older, better, more elevated traditions
of the Republican party, which General Grant seemed

HORACE GREELEY

to be fast drawing to the lower levels of self-aggrandize-
ment and power. Mr. Greeley wrote editorials every
day which told like sharp blows upon the consciousness of all the thousands of plain men the country-sides
through who looked to the *Tribune* for guidance as to
an oracle. It was no light matter to have such men
set against the administration.

It was the more embarrassing because there were
large matters of policy, as well as scattered items of
mistaken action and vague fears for the civil service,
upon which an opposition could concentrate. At the
heart of these was the disfranchisement of the white
men of the South. It was plain to see that the troubles
in the southern States arose out of the exclusion of
the better whites from the electoral suffrage no less
than from the admission of the most ignorant blacks.
It was no doubt in part because the South could not
use its real leaders in open political contest that impatient men and radicals had been driven to use secret
combination and all the ugly weapons of intimidation.
The processes of reconstruction were made by those
who managed them to depend as much upon withhold-
ing the suffrage from all who had participated with
any touch of leadership in secession as upon the use
of the negroes as voters and the radical amendment
of the southern constitutions; and it presently became
evident that there was a rapidly growing number of
thoughtful men in the Republican ranks who thought
it high time to grant a general amnesty and bring affairs
to a normal condition again in southern society. Mr.
Greeley was strongly of that opinion, and it took form
and bred concert of action rapidly enough to play a
determining part in the presidential campaign of 1872.

CARL SCHURZ

In 1870 the question had taken very definite form among the Republicans of Missouri, and the party had split asunder there into a radical and a liberal faction. The radicals wished for the present to maintain the disqualifications imposed by the constitution of the State upon those who had identified themselves with secession during the war; the liberals demanded "universal amnesty and universal enfranchisement," and won in the state elections. The leaders of the successful revolt were Mr. Benjamin Gratz Brown and Mr. Carl Schurz. Mr. Brown had been politician, editor, soldier, senator these twenty years, and with the success of his party became governor of the State. Mr. Schurz was a member of the Senate, a man but just turned of forty but bred since a lad to the rôle of aggressive liberal in politics,—an exile from his German home because of his participation in the revolutionary movements of 1849. He was an orator whom opponents not prepared to join frank issue found it prudent to avoid in open contest. Mr. Lincoln had named him minister to Spain in 1861, but he had preferred the field and entered the army; and at the close of the war had been sent by the legislature of Missouri to the Senate of the United States.

The "Liberal Republicans" of Missouri, thus led, called upon men of like views everywhere to join them, and their ranks for a little seemed to fill upon a scale which threatened to make them a formidable national faction. The form the presidential campaign of 1872 was to take was determined by their initiative. In May, 1872, a national convention of their partisans came together at Cincinnati, at the call of the Missouri leaders, and nominated Mr. Greeley for the presidency, Mr. Benjamin Gratz Brown for the vice presidency. These were nominations which the country found it hard to take seriously. Mr. Greeley's irregular genius, useful as it was in the trenchant statement of issues and the sharp challenge of opinion, was not of the kind prudent men were willing to see tried in the conduct of the government. He was too much a man of impulse, without poise or calculable lines of action. Mr. Brown the country did not know, except as a picturesque

BENJAMIN GRATZ BROWN

Missouri soldier and politician. The names of much more statesmanlike men had been proposed in the convention, but it had acted like a great mass meeting rather than like the organ of a party, upon impulse and hastily considered policy rather than with prudent forecast or real knowledge of the true grounds of

85

expediency. Its platform exhibited the same characteristics of half-formed opinion and a hurried compromise of interests. It condemned the existing administration as corrupt in its use of the patronage and absolutely disregardful of constitutional limitations in its use of power in the States, and demanded the "immediate and absolute removal of all disabilities imposed on account of the rebellion," in the belief that universal amnesty would "result in complete pacification in all parts of the country"; but its formulations of policy were vague and evasive. It was framed to please all elements of a mixed opposition, and to make as acceptable as possible its closing invitation to "all patriotic citizens, without regard to previous political affiliations," to join with its framers in purifying the government.

The Democratic convention, which met in Baltimore early in July, accepted both the platform and the candidates of the Cincinnati convention, though the Democratic leaders liked neither. The platform spoke no recognizable Democratic doctrine, except, indeed, in its advocacy of the maintenance of the public credit by a speedy return to specie payments, and the candidates were men whom no experienced politician could hope to see elected. But the split in the Republican ranks evidenced by the Cincinnati convention was the only sign anywhere visible to the Democratic leaders of a change in public sentiment likely to weaken the party in power. Without the coalition they knew themselves helpless; with it they hoped to make at least a show of strength. Such allies might be worth the weak candidates and the inconclusive declaration of principles that went with them. The "Liberal Republicans" had given form to the whole campaign, as they had expected.

The result was what every one who had the least sagacity in reading the signs of political weather perceived from the first it must be. The Democrats added but one hundred and thirty thousand to their popular vote of four years before, though the number of voters in the country had greatly increased and for the first time in the history of the government every State chose its electors by the direct suffrage of the people. The Republicans added six hundred thousand to their vote, and General Grant was elected for a second term by an overwhelming majority in the electoral college (286–63). The congressional elections which accompanied the choice of President gave the Republicans again, moreover, their accustomed two-thirds majority in both houses. All things stood as before; the opposition were yet a long way off from power. Mr. Greeley survived the elections but a few weeks. He had not seen how hopeless his candidacy was. He was turned of sixty and had been broken in health. All his years had been full of such keen and unremitting labor as robs a man at last of his elasticity. The sudden stroke of utter defeat, touched almost with farce, so that men laughed to see how complete it was, was more than he could bear. On the 29th of November, 1872, before the electors had voted, he died. The few votes that would have gone to him were given as the electors pleased to men who had been his allies in the novel coalition he had led.

And yet, though the coalition had failed, the Democrats were nearer their day of success than they dreamed. Within two years the Republican majority of nearly one hundred in the House of Representatives had been supplanted by a Democratic majority almost as large, and the men who had led the party of reconstruction found their season of mastery gone by. The country had begun to see with how radical a demoralization the war party it had trusted was beginning to be touched, and how impotent the amiable soldier they had put at the head of the government was to guide or better it. General Grant had found that the appointment of men to political office upon the recommendation of politicians and personal friends, though the friends were his own and the politicians men whom the country honored and whom he would have deemed it a reproach upon himself to distrust, was a very different matter from promoting officers tested under his own eye in camp and field. The leaders of Congress perceived plainly enough the movement of opinion out-of-doors, saw the service of the government steadily sinking to a lower level of efficiency, knew what influences were at work to debase it and what condemnation must come upon them should the use made of the patronage come fully to light. On the 3d of March, 1871, accordingly, they put through Congress an Act which authorized the President to frame and administer, through a commission, such rules as he thought best for the regulation of admissions to the civil service. The President accepted the Act with cordial approval, with an obvious sense of relief, indeed; and with complete indifference to the distress of the politicians proceeded to establish and enforce a system of competitive examinations for office. But the politicians were stronger in Congress than the President, and after two years of painful exclusion from the use of the patronage induced the houses

to withhold the appropriation necessary for the administration of the President's new system of appointment. They had not yet learned how hard a master
public opinion was to be in that matter.

Possibly the mere demoralization of the civil service
would not by itself have brought upon them the bitter
discipline of defeat which they presently underwent.
Other things went along with it which stirred the country more deeply; which made Congress itself seem corrupt and the party which controlled it without a watch-
ful sense of honor. The year 1869, in which General
Grant became President, had been marked by the completion of both the Central Pacific and the Union Pacific
railways, the two lines begun in 1863, the one eastward
from the Pacific, the other westward from the Missouri
River, which when completed at their point of junction
at last bound East and West together across the long
plains and the high passes of the Rockies upon which
so many a slow caravan had lost its way and its precious
freight of human lives. In 1867 the company which
had undertaken the construction of the Union Pacific
had acquired by purchase the charter of a corporation
organized in Pennsylvania in 1863 upon the model
of the great French *Société Générale du Crédit Mobilier,*
for the placing of loans, the handling of all marketable
stocks, and the transaction of a general banking business. The French company had come very near to
getting into its hands the whole brokerage business
and mercantile credit of France; the promoters of the
Union Pacific Railway bought out the Pennsylvania
company in order to obtain a suitable instrument for
conducting the financial operations connected with
their undertaking. Congress had made immense grants

in aid of the Pacific railway, regarding its construction as of no less importance to the government than to the commerce and material development of the country, because it would bind the two coasts of the continent which had hitherto been almost like separated countries together by a great highway along which authority and the influences of opinion could travel as well as trade. Its subsidies had taken the form of six *per cent.* gold bonds: $16,000 for every mile of rails upon the prairies or the coast plains beyond the mountains, from $32,000 to $48,000 for every mile through the passes of the mountains or the difficult country between range and range,—besides twenty-five million acres of public land along the line of the road.

Here was a perilously close connection between a great financial undertaking and legislation by Congress; and in the presidential campaign of 1872 it was openly charged by the Democrats that Mr. Colfax, the Vice President, Mr. Henry Wilson, the Vice President elect, the Speaker of the House of Representatives, and a number of senators and representatives had accepted gifts of Crédit Mobilier stock in consideration of legislative and other services to be rendered the company. Both houses appointed committees of investigation. The revelations which ensued filled the country with uneasiness and disgust. Against the more prominent officials accused no proof of conscious wrongdoing was found. Only two members of the House and a single member of the Senate were found to have deliberately engaged in transactions which touched their integrity and honor. But many a detail came to light which showed that members carried very easy-going consciences in such matters, accepted favors without look-

90

ing too curiously into their motive or significance, thought more often of their personal interests than of the public honor, and felt very slightly the responsibility

Schuyler Colfax   SCHUYLER COLFAX

of their posts of trust. It was open to any one who chose to believe that less had been told than had been covered up; that, with but a little more probing, it might have been possible to unearth many an unsavory intrigue. The discredit of the ruling party in the houses was steadily deepening.

The painful impressions left by the investigation were heightened by the deliberate action of the houses during the very session which saw it instituted and concluded. They did not scruple to pass an Act which increased the compensation of senators and representatives and which was made to apply retroactively to the sessions of the past two years,—an Act which the country very bluntly dubbed a "salary grab" and deemed quite in keeping with the reputation of a Congress which had censured but did not expel the members whom its own investigation had shown to be guilty of corrupt connection with the Crédit Mobilier.

Other impressions, well or ill founded, supervened which confirmed the country in its distrust of the men who were in control of affairs. In September, 1873, financial panic once more came upon the country with a rush, amidst abundant trade, amidst every sign of prosperity, when wages were good, employment readily found, factories busy, prices normal, money easy. Railways had been built too fast in the West. Within five years no less than $1,700,000,000 had been spent in railway construction. A Northern Pacific Railway was in course of construction, to be pushed forward through a new section of the country; and not a new Pacific railway only but shorter lines also by the score in regions where as yet there were no people, in order that parts of the country otherwise inaccessible might be opened up to quick settlement and profitable use. Such roads could not reasonably look to make a profit for twenty years to come. They were built with borrowed money. Their bonds filled every market, at home and abroad. Some new roads there were which were only extensions of older lines of established earning capacity; but the older portions could not earn enough to pay for the new. Certain as the prospects of profit were, when the country should grow and settlers come to dot the lines of rail with towns, flank them with farms, and put factories at every point of vantage, their construction was for the present purely speculative, and the processes of growth upon which they depended to keep them from bankruptcy could not be sufficiently hurried to save their credit. Early in September, 1873, the break began to come. One by one banking and brokerage firms in New York which had advanced money to western and Canadian railways began to announce their inability to meet their obligations. On the morning of the 18th Mr. Jay Cooke, the agent of the federal government, with $4,000,000 of deposits from all parts of the country and $15,000,000 of the paper of the Northern Pacific company, declared himself unable to meet his debts, and the "Street" knew that the end had come. Firm after firm, company after company, went to the wall, some of them reputed the strongest in the country, and a long, slow winter of panic ensued whose effects the business of the country was to feel for years to come.

Men who did not know how to reason upon such matters or how to distinguish the real forces that governed the credit of the country were inclined to attribute this sudden sweep of calamity across a money market apparently prosperous and at peace to the financial legislation of Congress. On the 12th of February, 1873, an Act had become law which, it was said, had "demonetized" silver and upset values. The

Act had dropped from the list of authorized coins the silver dollar of 412½ grains, which had hitherto been the standard silver dollar of the coinage, and had authorized,

JAY COOKE

in partial substitution, a "trade dollar" of 420 grains. No silver dollars of 412½ grains had been coined since 1808; since 1853 there had been no silver dollars in circulation; the Act simply made what was fact also law, and had passed without objection. But when the financial crisis of the autumn of 1873 came many persons recalled the "demonetization" of silver effected at the opening of the year, and made shrewd theories about the causes of a panic whose explanation was obvious and upon its face. The Republicans in Congress had had the ill fortune to alter the law of the currency upon the very eve of a financial disturbance, and those who did not like their conduct of the government and suspected them of more corruption than had been proved were at liberty to add this to the list of things they had done amiss, to the damage of the country. The congressional elections of the autumn of 1874 went heavily against them; the House was lost to the Democrats; their majority in the Senate was retained only because the Senate was guarded by its constitution against sudden change. The impressions of that autumn and the events of the next year lost them also the local elections in many of the northern States which had so far seemed their safe strongholds. Even Massachusetts chose a Democratic governor.

The country could not overlook the evidences of demoralization at Washington. In 1875 it was discovered that there was concerted action in the West between distillers and federal officials to defraud the government of large amounts in respect of the internal revenue tax on distilled spirits, a "whiskey ring," as the newspapers called it, which did not hesitate to use a portion of its fraudulent profits to make good its opportunity and its immunity by political corruption. Mr. Belknap, the Secretary of War, was accused of accepting bribes in dispensing the patronage of his Department, and, upon impeachment on that charge, resigned

his office as if in confession, to escape punishment.
Venality and fraud began on all hands to be suspected,
even where they did not exist, and mere inefficiency
began to irritate the country as if it were but a part of

WILLIAM WORTH BELKNAP

the general decadence of official honor. The President
himself saw how ill, how discreditably, and with how
incorrigible a tendency towards serious and even criminal
misconduct, the administrative branches of the public
service operated under his hand, and with the simplicity and frankness which were characteristic of him,—

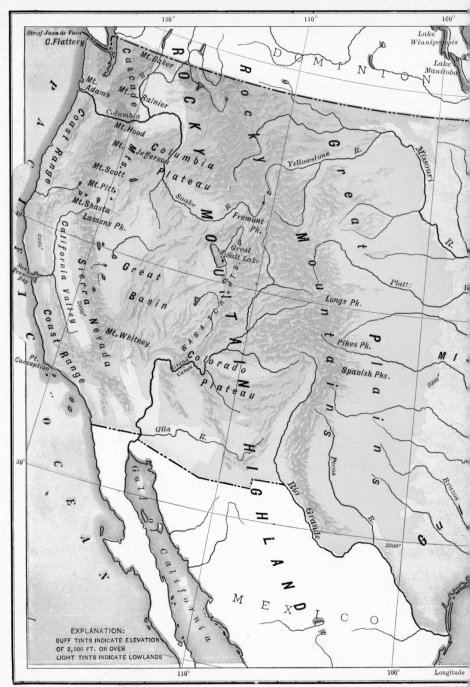

PHYSICAL FEATURES

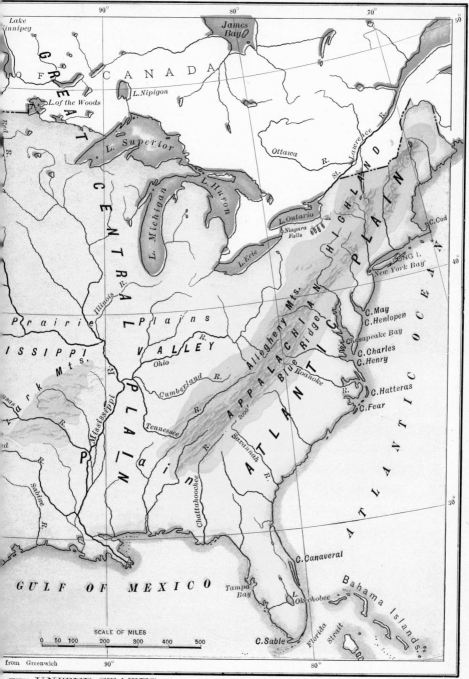

SCALE OF MILES

0   50 100   200   300   400   500

from Greenwich   90°   80°

THE UNITED STATES.

BURMAY & CO., N.Y.

Map labels:
Lake Winnipeg
GREAT CANADA
James Bay
L. of the Woods
L. Nipigon
Ottawa R.
Red R.
L. Superior
L. Michigan
L. Huron
St. Lawrence R.
L. Ontario
Niagara Falls
L. Erie
C. Cod
GREAT CENTRAL
HIGHLAND
PLAIN
LONG I.
New York Bay
Illinois R.
Prairie Plains
C. May
C. Henlopen
Chesapeake Bay
MISSISSIPPI
VALLEY
Ohio R.
Appalachian Mts.
Allegheny Mts.
Blue Ridge
C. Charles
C. Henry
Ozark Mts.
Cumberland R.
Roanoke R.
C. Hatteras
Arkansas R.
Mississippi R.
Tennessee R.
C. Fear
APPALACHIAN
2000
ATLANTIC OCEAN
Red R.
Savannah R.
Sabine R.
Chattahoochee R.
PLAIN
GULF OF MEXICO
Tampa Bay
C. Canaveral
Bahama Islands
L. Okeechobee
Florida Strait
C. Sable

the simplicity and frankness which unscrupulous politicians played upon to betray him,—acknowledged his failure and longed for release from duties in the performance of which he knew that he had blundered. His eight years of power had cost his party its predominance.

It was not the condition of the civil service alone, however, or the mere alarm of the country at the too frequent disclosures of malfeasance in office which brought the ascendency of the Republicans to an end. Congress did its part to make it plain that nothing but blunders were to be expected from the political legislation of the men who had devised and forced to their execution the measures of reconstruction. On Christmas day, 1868, President Johnson had proclaimed full pardon and amnesty for all who had participated in secession, without reserve or exception, and by an Act of the 2d of May, 1872, Congress had removed the political disabilities imposed by the third section of the Fourteenth Amendment from all who had served the Confederate States, except only those who had left the Congress of the United States or the judicial, military, or naval service of the federal government, the headship of an executive Department or the post of minister at a foreign court to take part with the seceding States. But, though they thus cleared away the more abnormal obstructions to the return of settled peace and a natural order of life at the South, the congressional leaders could not keep their hands from the race question. Mr. Sumner, in particular, was insistent that the negroes should be given imperative federal law for their support in the assertion of their social no less than of their political rights; and in February, 1875, at last had his way, though he did not live to see it. A bill passed which gave the federal courts the authority, by appropriate process and penalty, to enforce the right of negroes to accommodation in public inns, theatres, railway carriages, and schools, and to service upon all juries, upon the same footing as white persons. The Act became law on the 1st of March, three days before the expiration of the term of the last House of Representatives the Republicans were effectually to control for fifteen years. It was the older leaders' last Act for creating friction at the South. For eight years it was to fail utterly of accomplishing its object and yet to work its work of irritation, to be set aside at last by the Supreme Court (1883) as an invasion of the legal field of the States which no portion of the constitution, new or old, could be made to sustain.

The reconstruction of the southern States had been the undoing of the Republican party. The course of carpet bag rule did not run smooth. Every election fixed the attention of the country upon some serious question of fraud or violence in the States where northern adventurers and negro majorities were in control. Congress could not remove the political disabilities of the southern white men without increasing their power at the polls and cutting at the foundations of Republican rule in the South; and yet, though the white voters were disfranchised, in at least three of the southern States Republican rule was maintained only by direct aid from Washington,—and sometimes at the point of the bayonet. General Grant had grown infinitely impatient that there should come every year, from State after State, calls for troops to keep the Republican governments at the South in their place of power. "The

whole public are tired out with these annual autumnal
outbreaks in the South," he said, in refusing troops to
the governor of Mississippi, "and the great majority
are ready now to condemn any interference on the part
of the government. I heartily wish that peace and
good order may be restored without issuing the proclamation. But, if it is issued, I shall instruct the commanders
of the forces to have no child's play." Here was the
right feeling of the man and the grim firmness of the
soldier. He was not mistaken as to the feeling of the
country; and though he withheld his hand where he
could, there was military interference enough to ex-
asperate that opinion to the utmost. Before his term
was out the white voters of the South had rallied strong
enough in every State except South Carolina, Florida,
and Louisiana to take their governments out of the
hands of the men who were preying upon them. That
they had done it by methods which only an almost
revolutionary state of society justified no one doubted:
by keeping the negroes away from the polls by every
form of intimidation, by forceable interference with
their rights when necessary, by every expedient, whether
of law or of subtile management, that promised them
mastery; but they had triumphed, and there was at
least an end of chronic revolution.

But in Louisiana, in Florida, and in South Carolina,
though desperately beset, the Republicans had, by
desperate means, kept their hold upon the governments
they had made. The troops of the United States were
first used to adjust the contest in Louisiana. The
revised constitution of Louisiana, revised in the interest of the congressional plan of reconstruction, provided, as most of the new southern constitutions did,

for the determination of the results of all elections by a returning board so constituted as to be always under the control of the existing administration of the State. That board had the right to reject, without judicial process and upon its own mere opinion, the votes of all counties or precincts where force or fraud had been employed; and it used that power to check the rising Democratic vote wherever it seriously threatened the supremacy of those in authority. Its surveillance went smoothly enough so long as the Republicans were themselves united; but the Republicans of Louisiana had fallen apart into factions, vacancies upon the returning board had been made and filled by removals and appointments, amidst disputes and contests of legal right, until there were at last two boards instead of one, and before the matter was quieted three, each of which claimed to be the legal returning board of the State. The result of the election of the autumn of 1872 turned upon their rival claims. Over one the Democrats had got control by coalition with the "liberal" wing of the Republicans; another declared the Republican state officers and the Republican candidates for the state legislature elected, and federal aid was asked to carry its judgment into effect. A committee of Congress, sent down to investigate the matter, found it impossible to disentangle the hopeless quarrel; Congress failed to pass the only measure of relief its leaders were able to think of, a bill providing for a new election; and the President recognized and installed the Republican governor.

It was not an affair which either party could look back upon with complacency, but the Republicans took the greater discredit from it, and the country grew very restive. A committee of the Senate reported that the district judge of the United States for the District of Louisiana had undoubtedly gone far beyond the scope of his power and acted in "flagrant disregard of his

SITTING BULL

duty" in his use of writs of injunction issued in aid of the faction which the President sustained. Some unsavory intrigue had been uncovered at almost every step of the investigation. Moreover, the action of the President was no settlement of the difficulty.

It left the State in a heightened temper of revolution. Riots accompanied the efforts of the questionable government he set up to enforce its authority. In September, 1874, the partisans of Mr. McEnery, the leader of the combined Democrats and "liberal" Republicans, rose in arms, put every officer of his opponent's administration from his place, and assumed control of the government. Again federal troops intervened, and the ousted officers were reinstated. Nice compromises, difficult to maintain and satisfactory to nobody, had to be devised to keep the peace until there should be another trial of strength in the election of a governor at the polls.

The summer of 1876 was darkened by a tragic war with the Indians of the far West. In 1874 gold had been discovered in the Black Hills which lay upon the border line of Wyoming and Dakota, and the rush of settlers and miners thither had exasperated the Sioux tribes to take the war path. Their chief was Sitting Bull, whom the troops of the United States were to find an opponent to put them on their mettle. Gathering his forces within the secluded valley of the Little Big Horn by the upper waters of the Yellowstone, where he could best mask his strength, he struck first at one and then at another of the three small bodies of soldiers sent to converge upon him. One he forced back; another he effectually checked; part of the third he trapped and utterly destroyed. General Terry, coming against him from Bismarck, sent General Custer forward with the seventh cavalry to go round about and attack him at the rear; and on the 25th of June, riding with five companies hard upon the camp, Custer rode into a death trap. The Indians swarmed around him in numbers which utterly overwhelmed and completely cut him off from retreat, and not a man came away to tell the tale. The other seven companies of the regiment were not at hand to fight with them or to give them succor, and found themselves obliged, when at last they came up,

GEORGE ARMSTRONG CUSTER

to fortify a bluff near at hand as a place of safety and retreat until they should themselves be succored and relieved. The forces of the government gathered at last to complete the work so ill begun, and the Indians retired to the mountains; but it took much painful fight-ing, and many toilsome marches, prosecuted through all the long autumn and the winter itself, to bring them to terms; and Sitting Bull slipped through their hands across the northern border at last.

Meanwhile the presidential election of 1876 had come and the full harvest of the mischief done in the reconstruction of the South was being reaped. The Democrats nominated Mr. Samuel J. Tilden, a man who had shown his quality as governor of the State of New York and won the respect of all thoughtful men, alike for his integrity and for his ability. The Republicans nominated Mr. Rutherford B. Hayes, who had won his place in the public confidence as an officer of volunteers in the war for the Union, as a member of the House of Representatives, and as governor of Ohio. Both men stood removed from the passionate contests of the period of reconstruction. Their candidacy put the emphasis of party contest as much as might be upon the issues of the new day rather than of the old. But the immediate past was a weight upon the fortunes of the Republicans; the country had turned with evident distrust from the work of confusion they had wrought. Again, as in 1874, Democratic majorities seemed to sweep the country. Only the confusion the Republicans themselves had brought about saved them from utter defeat. State elections had been held, as usual, in most of the States at the same time that presidential electors were chosen, and once again the result of the elections in Louisiana, Florida, and South Carolina was in dispute. The electoral votes of all of these States were necessary for the election of Mr. Hayes. Mr. Tilden had carried Connecticut, New York, New Jersey, Delaware, Maryland, Indiana, and Missouri, as well as the ten southern States whose votes were not in dis-

RUTHERFORD BIRCHARD HAYES

pute; one hundred and eighty-four electoral votes were secured for him beyond a doubt, and one hundred and eighty-five constituted a majority. A single additional electoral vote would bring him into the presidency, and it seemed possible that at least one might be added to his reckoning by Oregon. There three Republican electors had undoubtedly been chosen, but one of them was thought to have been ineligible under the law, and the Democratic governor had appointed in his stead the next candidate on the poll, a Democrat, and given him his certificate.

In the South nineteen electoral votes were in dispute. In Louisiana there had, apparently, been a clear majority of Democratic votes cast at the polls, alike for presidential electors and for governor and state legislators; but once again the returning board, which was in the hands of Republicans, had turned a Democratic into a Republican majority by rejecting the votes of precincts in which it declared fraud or intimidation to have been used. Certificates had been given to the Republican presidential electors, accordingly, and again a Republican state government had been set up by force of authority. But again the Democrats had refused to yield. They had set up, on their own part, a Democratic administration, and Mr. Nicholls, whom they claimed to have elected governor, gave certificates to the Democratic electors. In Florida the vote had been very close indeed, and turned upon the votes of a single county. The returning board of the State had but a single Democratic member, the Attorney General, and the majority of the board had given the vote of the State to the Republicans. The Attorney General had issued certificates over his own signature to the Democratic

Samuel J. Tilden SAMUEL JONES TILDEN

electors. In South Carolina federal troops had in many places guarded the polls, and federal troops had assisted the Republican leaders of the State to put the governor and state legislators whom they claimed to have elected into office; but the Democrats claimed that their candidates had in fact been chosen, notwithstanding the obstructions to free voting created by the presence of troops and the interference of federal supervisors acting under the "Force Bills" of 1870 and 1871; inaugurated their own governor, General Wade Hampton, a distinguished cavalry commander of the Confederacy; and set up their own legislature. General Hampton issued certificates of election to the Democratic presidential electors.

All the country saw, with an instant thrill of misgiving, how perilous a situation was thus created. Here were double returns from three States in a presidential election, and the decision which should be chosen must determine the election. One vote out of the twenty in dispute, though it were only the single questionable vote of Oregon, would give the presidency to the Democrats. The control of the government turned upon the action of the houses when they should come to count the votes in joint session. The House of Representatives was Democratic, the Senate Republican; there was no hope that they could agree. No one could confidently say, though he put partisanship aside and held his judgment at the nicest poise, upon which side the right lay in the disputed southern elections. It was plain enough that in any case the returning boards would have given the vote to the Republicans, whatever the face of the returns, so long as the men for whom they acted felt that they could count upon the support of the Executive at Washington in the maintenance of their authority. It was equally clear, on the other hand, that there were all but indisputable evidences

W. Hampton WADE HAMPTON

of fraud or at the least irregularity in the votes upon which the Democrats relied. In South Carolina serious riots had occurred whose avowed object had been the intimidation of the negroes. The country had grown very impatient, as General Grant said, of seeing governments maintained at the South by federal arms, and wished very heartily to see the hand of the federal Executive withdrawn, come what come might; and yet it was not as clear as could be wished that this was the occasion for their legitimate overthrow.

What the country had really to fear was, not the difficulty of the problem as a question of justice, but the passion of parties, the danger that those who stood at the front of party counsels would seek the success of their party by some intrigue, even by some stroke of violence. Foreseeing a certain deadlock of the houses when it should come to a counting of the votes, there was talk among the more headlong and reckless partisans of each side of taking the law into their own hands. There were signs almost of civil war in the air for a few troubled weeks of that anxious autumn.

But it was never really likely it would come to that. Men trained in the temper of American institutions had never thought to settle a constitutional difficulty after that fashion. Congress listened very willingly to counsels of compromise and moderation. It was agreed that an electoral commission should be constituted, which should consist of five members of the House, three Democrats and two Republicans, five members of the Senate, three Republicans and two Democrats, two Democrats and two Republicans from the supreme bench of the United States, and an additional Justice from the same court selected by the four Justices named in the bill; and that to that commission should be referred every question in dispute. Such a commission was undoubtedly an extra-constitutional body, and its decisions disappointed the

country of any display of judicial impartiality it may
have hoped for from it. Mr. Justice Bradley, who was
chosen by his fellow Justices of the commission to be
the fifteenth member of the tribunal, voted in every
instance in favor of the Republican claims, as did every

JOSEPH P. BRADLEY

other member of the commission, whether judge, senator,
or representative, whose affiliations were with the Republican party. Every Democrat of the commission
voted in favor of the claims of the Democratic managers.
Every question submitted was settled by a vote of eight
to seven. But there was at least a settlement, which
no one dreamed of disputing or attempting to annul.

General Grant gave way to Mr. Hayes, and the government remained in the hands of the Republicans.

To Mr. Hayes the tacit obligations of the situation were plain. He withdrew the federal troops from the South. The Republican governments of Louisiana and South Carolina were dissolved, and the Democratic governments which had claimed the election quietly took their place. The supreme court of Florida obliged the returning board of the State to accept the returns which had come to them from the disputed county, and a Democratic government came there also into power. The era of reconstruction was at an end.

The quiet figure of the retiring President began to seem almost at once like a figure lingering out of an age gone by. The honest, simple-hearted soldier had not added prestige to the presidential office. He himself knew that he had failed, that the administrative scandals, the stain of corruption, of intrigue, of malversation, the appearance as if of a group of personal allies bent upon their own aggrandizement rather than of a body of public servants devoted to the honest conduct of the nation's business, which had marked his management of the executive office must always stand as proof that he ought never to have been made President. But the corruption had not touched him. He was unstained. Every one who thought justly of the matter attributed his failure rather to his very honesty and simplicity of nature than to any fault of will. His trustfulness had betrayed him; his desire to be faithful to his friends had led him to shield knaves. He had thought other men as honest, as straightforward as himself. He had come to a great office untrained in affairs. Men's eyes followed his retreating figure with respect, with

R.B.Hayes

veneration, with deep affection, and forgot that he had been duped by politicians; remembered only that he had been the successful leader of the armies of the republic.

Authorities. All the larger and more systematic histories of the country stop short of times so recent as those covered by this chapter. Neither is it any longer feasible to distinguish general authorities from contemporary accounts. All accounts of a time so recent are contemporary. We have for general guidance Judson S. Landon's *Constitutional History and Government of the United States*, Alexander Johnston's *American Politics*, the same author's admirable articles on the several topics here treated of, such as *Reconstruction*, the *Ku Klux*, *Crédit Mobilier*, etc., in Lalor's *Cyclopaedia of Political Science, Political Economy, and United States History*, John Clark Ridpath's popular *History of the United States*, John W. Burgess's *Reconstruction and the Constitution*, Edward Channing's *Student's History of the United States*, Edward Stanwood's *History of the Presidency*, Appleton's *Annual Cyclopaedia*, Edward McPherson's *Handbook of Politics*, issued in biennial volumes, except in 1870, from 1868 to 1894, Scribner's *Statistical Atlas of the United States*, to 1880, William A. Dunning's *Essays on the Civil War and Reconstruction*, G. W. Williams's *History of the Negro Race in America*, W. H. Barnes's *History of the Thirty-ninth Congress*, Albert Bushnell Hart's *Foundations of American Foreign Policy*, and many valuable articles scattered through the volumes of the *Atlantic Monthly* (especially a series on Reconstruction which appeared in 1901), the *North American Review*, *The Forum*, *The Nation*, and the *Political Science Quarterly*.

Among the more important *memoirs* are James G. Blaine's *Twenty Years of Congress*, S. S. Cox's *Three Decades of Federal Legislation, 1855 to 1885*, Hugh McCulloch's *Men and Measures of Half a Century*, John Sherman's *Recollections of Forty Years in the House, Senate, and Cabinet*, Dabney Herndon Maury's *Recollections of a Virginian*, Bishop R. H. Wilmer's *Recent Past from a Southern Standpoint*, Reuben Davis's *Recollections of Mississippi and Mississippians*, and G. W. Julian's *Political Recollections*.

Adam Badeau's *Grant in Peace*, A. R. Conkling's *Life and Letters of Roscoe Conkling*, John Bigelow's *Life of Samuel J. Tilden*, Albert Bushnell Hart's *Salmon P. Chase* in the *American*

Statesmen Series, and Moorfield Storey's *Charles Sumner,* in the
same *Series,* cover parts of the period from the point of view of
the several men of whom they treat.

Mr. Hilary A. Herbert's *Why the Solid South?* and Mr. William
Garrott Brown's *The Lower South in American History* throw a
great deal of light upon the time in regard to the affairs and the
sentiment of the South; Mr. J. Lawrence Laughlin's *History of
Bimetallism in the United States* and Professor F. W. Taussig's
Silver Situation in the United States and *Tariff History of the
United States,* and Mr. A. S. Bolles's *Financial History of the
United States,* furnish excellent summaries of financial and fiscal
conditions; Mr. Carroll D. Wright's *Industrial Evolution of the
United States* sketches the development of industry and invention,
and Mr. David A. Wells's *Recent Economic Changes* the altered
economic conditions; Mr. Lauros G. McConachie's *Congressional
Committees* and Miss M. P. Follett's *The Speaker of the House
of Representatives* discuss the transformations of Congress and
its relations to public business; and Mr. Henry Jones Ford's *Rise
and Growth of American Politics* affords one of the best phil-
osophical analyses of the general history of parties, party organization, and party control, anywhere to be found.

The *sources* are in the *Journals* of Congress, the *Congressional
Record,* the House and Senate *Documents,* the *Messages and Papers
of the Presidents,* and the periodical press of the time.

CHAPTER II

RETURN TO NORMAL CONDITIONS

WITH the coming in of Mr. Hayes the whole air of politics seemed to change. Democratic critics of the administration were inclined to dwell with a good deal of acidity upon the flagrant inconsistency of the President's course in first using the questionable governments of Louisiana and South Carolina to get his office and then forthwith repudiating them and bringing about their immediate downfall by withdrawing the federal troops upon whose presence and support they relied for their existence; and his friends could urge only that the constitution provides that presidential electors shall be "appointed" by each State "in such manner as the legislature thereof may direct," and that it might with perfect consistency be argued that the legislatures of the southern States could commit to their returning boards the right to choose presidential electors while at the same time maintaining that those boards ought not to be sustained in the virtual selection of state governors and legislatures as well. But, in any case, whether consistent or inconsistent, the President's action had brought grateful peace. Almost at once affairs wore a normal aspect again. The process of reconstruction, at least, had reached its unedifying end, and the hands of political leaders were free to take up the history of the country where it had been broken off in 1861. Instead of the quick, resistless despatch of party measures from session to session by congressional majorities which even the President's veto could not check or defeat, there had come a breathing space in which no party was supreme and the slow and moderate ways of compromise and accommodation were once again vouchsafed the country, at last quite out of breath with the pace to which it had been forced in its affairs. Not for fourteen years, from the elections of 1875 to those of 1889, were either Democrats or Republicans to control both Congress and the Executive. There was leisure from passion; men could look about them deliberately and without excitement and note how the country had changed.

It was no longer the country of 1861. Sixteen years, mixed of war which forced industry to a quick, almost abnormal development and of peace that came like a release of energies cramped, pent up, uneasy, had brought something like an industrial revolution with them. The South was of a sudden added as a modern economic force to the nation. Her old system of labor, which had shut her in to a virtual isolation, was destroyed; she was open at last to the labor of the world and was to enter with all her resources the industrial life from which she had so long held off. The great Appalachian region which stretched its mighty highlands from Pennsylvania through Maryland, the Virginias, Kentucky, Tennessee, and the Carolinas full seven hundred miles into Alabama and Georgia, and which spread its broad surfaces of mountain, valley, and plateau one hundred and fifty miles by the way upon either hand, geologists knew to be an almost unbroken coal field, it might be thirty-nine thousand square

A TYPICAL SCENE IN THE APPALACHIAN MOUNTAINS

miles in area. Upon its skirts and in the broken country to the east and west of it iron also abounded, and mineral deposits which no man had looked into. The world still needed the southern cotton and tobacco, and before the first crude processes of reconstruction were over the cotton fields were once more producing almost as much as they had yielded in 1860, the year of greatest abundance ere the war came on,—so readily had free labor taken the place of slave. The industrial development of the South had been joined to that of the rest of the country, and for the first time since the modern industrial age set in capitalists turned to her for investment and the enterprises that bring wealth and power.

And what was for the South as yet but an exciting prospect and confident hope was for the North already a reality. The war had been a supreme test of economic vitality, and the States of the North and West had emerged from it stronger than they went into it. Almost every industry that yielded the necessaries of modern life and action had felt and responded to its quickening compulsion; and when peace came manufacturers but looked about them for wider markets, better and cheaper processes, a broader scope of operation. Artificial stimulation in the shape of heavy tariff duties had been added to the natural stimulation of the time and of the rapid and healthy growth of the nation. Congress had taxed almost every article of use in the country to support the war, and had added to the innumerable direct taxes which it imposed an enormously expanded system of duties on imports. It had done so in part to offset the direct taxes, to enable the manufacturers, who had to pay large sums to the

INTERIOR OF THE MAIN BUILDING AT THE PHILADELPHIA CENTENNIAL EXHIBITION

government on the articles they made, to keep the market nevertheless against the importers; but it had made the duties much higher than that consideration taken alone made necessary. It had raised them to a point that made profit, very great profit, certain to accrue to the manufacturer. No considerable body of manufacturers asked for such "protection" that did not get it, and as much of it as they asked for, though it reduced the revenues of the government to grant it. Hardly a month went by while the war lasted that Congress did not add a new duty or increase an old one, and every industry was nursed to make the most of itself in the home markets, until its undisputed monopoly there as against foreign manufactures gave it wide margins of profit of which to avail itself in underselling competitors in the markets of the world.

The country got visible proof of its extraordinary material progress at its Centennial Exhibition in Philadelphia. The last year of General Grant's presidency was the centennial year of the independence of the United States, and the anniversary was celebrated by a great international industrial exposition at the city of Philadelphia, where the Congress had sat which took counsel for the young republic at its birth. All the greater commercial and industrial nations were represented in its exhibits. Foreign governments responded very promptly to the invitation to lend their aid in securing its success, among the rest the government of Great Britain, whose defeat in arms the great fair was meant to celebrate. The presence of her official commissioners made it a festival of reconciliation. America's own bitter war of civil revolution also was over, and a time of healing at hand. The thronging crowds at Philadelphia, the gay and spacious buildings, the peaceable power of the world's workmen exhibited upon every hand spoke of good will and the brotherhood of nations, where there was no rivalry but the rivalry to serve and to enrich mankind.

It was significant for America that objects of beauty marked everywhere among those exhibits the refinement and the ennobling art of the world. Throughout all the long hundred years in which they had been building a nation Americans had shown themselves children of utility, not of art. Beauty they had neglected. Everything they used showed only the plain, unstudied lines of practical serviceability. Grace was not in their thought, but efficiency. The very houses they built, whether for homes or for use in their business, showed how little thought they gave to the satisfaction of the eye. Their homes were for the most part of wood and the perishable material hardly justified costly ornament or elaborate design; and yet the men of the colonial time, keeping still some of the taste of an older world, had given even their simple frame dwellings a certain grace and dignity of line, and here and there a detail, about some doorway or the columns of a stately porch, which rewarded the eye. Builders of the later time had forgotten the elder canons of taste and built without artistic perception of form even when they built elaborately and at great cost. The same plainness, the same hard lines of mere serviceability were to be seen in almost everything the country made. The things to be seen at Philadelphia, gathered from all the world, awakened it to a new sense of form and beauty. Foreign governments had generously sent priceless works of painting and sculpture over sea to give distinction to the galleries of the Exhibition. Private citizens and local museums also had freely loaned their chief art treasures. Everywhere there was some touch of beauty, some suggested grace of form. Visitors poured by the million across the grounds and through the buildings of the Exhibition, out of every State and region of the country, and the impressions they received were never wholly obliterated. Men and women of all sorts, common and gentle alike, had from that day a keener sense of what was fitted to please the eye. The pride of life and of great success that came with the vision of national wealth and boundless resources to be got from the countless exhibits of farm and factory had in it also some touch of corrected taste, some impulse of suitable adornment. Men knew afterwards that that had been the dawn of an artistic renaissance in America which was to put her architects and artists alongside the modern masters of beauty and redeem the life of her people from its ugly severity.

That great fair might also serve to mark the shifting stress of the nation's life. Its emphasis was henceforth, for at least a generation, to rest on economic, not upon political or constitutional, questions. The changing character of public affairs had been indicated as early as the presidential campaign of 1872. That campaign had witnessed not only the emergence of the "Liberal Republican" party, made up upon the questions of political amnesty and a thorough reform of the civil service of the government, but also the creation of a "Labor Reform" party whose programme said little or nothing of the ordinary political issues of the day and spoke mainly of the relations of capital and labor, of the legal limitation of the hours of daily work, of the need of a currency which should render the people less subject to the power of the banks, of the control of the railways and the telegraph lines by the federal government, of the disposal of the public lands. The convention of the new party had been made up chiefly of trades union bosses and political free lances, but it had brought delegates together out of seventeen States

HORTICULTURAL HALL AT THE PHILADELPHIA CENTENNIAL EXHIBITION

and was an unmistakable sign of the times. The workingmen of the country were about to bestir themselves to make their power felt in the choices of government and law. In 1876 an "Independent National" party came upon the field, to make the issue of legal tender notes by the government, in place alike of gold and of silver, the chief point of its protest against the programmes of the two regular parties. To the country it was known as the "Greenback" party. The notes

which it demanded should be issued were to be practically irredeemable, being convertible, not into gold
or silver, but "into United States obligations merely."
It was practically repeating the demand of the Labor
Reform party of four years before for "a purely national
circulating medium, based on the faith and resources
of the nation, and issued directly to the people without the intervention of any system of banking corporations," in order that there might be established "a just
standard of the distribution of capital and labor."

On all hands there was manifest a growing uneasiness
because of the apparent rise of monopolies and the
concentration of capital in the hands of comparatively
small groups of men who seemed to be in a position to
control at their pleasure the productive industries of
the country; because of the power of the railways to
determine by discriminating rates what sections of
the country, what industries, what sorts of products
and of manufactures should be accorded the easiest
access to the markets; because of the increase in the
cost of the necessary tools of industry and of all manu-
factured goods through the operation of the tariff,—
the inequitable clogs which seemed to many to be put
by the law itself upon the free and wholesome rivalries
of commerce and production. The farmers of the West
and South, no less than the workingmen of the industrial
East, had begun, close upon the heels of the war, to
organize themselves for the protection and advancement of their own special interests, to which the programmes of the political parties paid little heed. Between 1872 and 1875 the local "granges" of a secret order
known as the Patrons of Industry had multiplied in a
very significant manner, until their membership rose

IN YELLOWSTONE PARK. GRAND CAÑON, POINT LOOKOUT, AND GREAT FALLS

to quite a million and a half and was spread over almost the entire Union. It was the purpose of the order to promote by every proper means the interests of the farmers of the country, though it was no part of its plan to agitate questions of politics, put candidates for office into the field at elections, or use its gathering power to determine the fate of parties. Politicians, nevertheless, found means to use it,—felt obliged to use it because they feared to let it act for itself. Its discussions turned often on questions of transportation, upon the railways and their power to make or ruin; it was but a short step in such a field from an association for mutual protection and advice to a political party organized for the control of legislation.

"Grangers" were not always to be held off, therefore, by their prudent leaders from using their numbers and their ready concert of action to further or defeat the ambitions of particular groups of politicians; and even while their granges grew other organizations of farmers came into existence whose aims were frankly and openly political. About the time of Mr. Hayes's accession to the presidency independent associations began to make their appearance in the South and in the West, under the name of the "Farmers' Alliance," whose common object it was to oppose monopoly and the power of money in public affairs in the interest of those who had neither the use of capital nor the protection of tariffs. The first "Alliance" made its appearance in Texas, to prevent the wholesale purchase of the public lands of the State by private individuals. The organization spread into other southern States, and with its extension went also an enlargement of its programme of reform. Almost at the same time

LOGGING IN THE MINNESOTA PINES.

a "National Farmers' Alliance" was established in Illinois which quickly extended its organization into Wisconsin, Minnesota, Iowa, Kansas, and Dakota. Many sorts of reform commended themselves to the leaders of the movement, north and south: chief among them, government control of the means of transportation, the entire divorce of the government from the banks, and a paper currency issued directly to the people on the security of their land,—some escape from the power of the money lenders and of the great railways, and a war upon monopolies. These were vague purposes, and the means of reform proposed showed the thinking of crude and ignorant minds; but politicians felt with evident concern that new, it might be incontrollable, forces had begun to play through the matters they handled, and that it must presently be harder than ever to calculate the fortunes of parties at the polls. They perceived how difficult and delicate a task it must prove to keep the tacit pledges of the protective system

127

to the manufacturers and give the free capital of the country the proper support of government and yet satisfy the classes now astir in these new associations of laborers and farmers, whose distress was as real as their programmes of reform were visionary.

There was a significance in these new movements which did not lie upon the surface. New questions had become national and were being uncomfortably pressed upon the attention of national party leaders because the attitude of the country towards the national government had been subtly changed by the events of war and reconstruction. The war had not merely roused the spirit of nationality, until then but half conscious, into vivid life and filled every country-side of the North and West with a new ardor for that government which was greater than the government of States, the government upon which the unity and prestige of the nation itself depended. It had also disclosed the real foundations of the Union; had shown them to be laid, not in the constitution, its mere formal structure, but upon deep beds of conviction and sentiment. It was not a theory of lawyers that had won when the southern Confederacy was crushed, but the passionate beliefs of an efficient majority of the nation, to whom the constitution was but a partial expression of the ideals which underlay their common life. While the war lasted the forms of the constitution had been with difficulty observed, had, indeed, again and again given way that the whole force of the nation might run straight and unimpeded to meet the exigencies of the portentous struggle. Mr. Lincoln had wielded an authority known to none of his predecessors. There had been moments when it seemed almost as if all constitutional rules

George Wm Curtis.

GEORGE WILLIAM CURTIS

were suspended and law superseded by force in order that the contest for nationality might not halt or be hindered. And when the war was over the process of reconstruction showed the same method and temper. No scrupulous care was taken to square what was done in the South with the law of the constitution. The will of Congress operated there like that of an absolute parliament, even while the lawyers of the houses who supported the measures of reconstruction were protesting that the States they were handling like provinces were still members of the Union. The internal affairs of the humbled States were altered at the pleasure of the congressional leaders, and yet it was said that they had not been put forth from the pale of the constitution.

It was inevitable that the whole spirit of affairs should be profoundly affected by such events. A revolution had been wrought in the consciousness and point of view of the nation. Parts had shifted and the air had changed. Conceptions were radically altered with regard to Congress, with regard to the guiding and compulsive efficacy of national legislation and the relation of the life of the land to the supremacy of the federal law-making body. A government which had been in its whole spirit federal had, almost of a sudden, become national, alike in method and in point of view. The national spirit which the war had aroused to bring this about had long been a-making. Many a silent force which grew quite unobserved from generation to generation, in quiet times of wholesome peace and mere increase of nature, had been slowly breeding the thoughts which had now sprung so vividly into consciousness. The very growth of the nation, the very lapse of time and uninterrupted habit of united action, the mere mixture and movement and distribution of populations, the mere accretions of policy, the mere consolidation of interests, had been building and strengthening new tissue of nationality the years through, and drawing links stronger than links of steel about the invisible body of common thought and purpose which is the substance of nations. When the great crisis of secession came men knew at once how their spirits were ruled, men of the South as well as men of the North,—in what institutions, in what conceptions of government their blood was fixed to run; and a great and instant readjustment took place, which was for the South, the minority, practically the readjustment of conquest and fundamental revolution, but which was for the North nothing more than an awakening.

There had been no constitutional forms for such a business. For several years, consequently, Congress had been permitted to do by statute what, under the older conceptions of the federal law, could properly be done only by constitutional amendment. The necessity for that gone by, it was suffered to embody in the constitution what it had already enacted and put into operation as law, not by the free will of the country at large, but by the compulsions of mere force exercised upon a minority whose assent was necessary to the formal completion of its policy. The result restored, practically entire, the forms of the constitution; but not before new methods and irregular, the methods of majorities but not the methods of law, had been openly learned and practised, and learned in a way not likely to be forgotten. It was not merely the economic

changes of a new age, therefore, that inclined laborers
and farmers to make programmes of reform which they
purposed to carry out through the instrumentality of
Congress; it was also this new conception of the supremacy of the federal law-making body, of the potency
of all legislation enacted at Washington. The country
was turning thither for all sorts of relief, for assistance
in all parts of its life.

And yet other changes had come upon the government at Washington which rendered it a less serviceable instrument of use than it had once been. Nothing
had become more emphasized during the reconstruction
period than the virtual supremacy of the houses over
the President in all matters outside the field of war
and foreign affairs,—in foreign affairs even, when
they chose. No President since General Jackson had
been the real leader of his party until Lincoln; and
Lincoln's term had made no permanent difference in
the practices established since Jackson's day. It had
been a time apart. In war the Executive was of course
at the front of affairs; Congress but sustained it in the
conduct of exigent business which, in the very nature
of the case, it could not itself undertake. Parties, too,
were silent; the nation had put ordinary questions
of policy aside. No man could say how Mr. Lincoln
might have ruled the counsels of his party in times
of quiet peace. With Mr. Johnson in the presidency,
Congress and the Executive had swung violently apart.
General Grant had not brought them together. He
was no party man and no statesman, had been bred
to affairs of another kind, let constructive suggestion
alone, made no pretence of political leadership. Under
the strong will of Mr. Thaddeus Stevens a real primacy

in affairs had been created for the men who led upon the floor of the houses, and old tendencies had been confirmed.

During the first days of the government, while the old order held and English traditions were still strong, the President had been the central figure in affairs,— partly because delicate questions of foreign policy pressed constantly for solution, partly because the early Presidents were chosen from the ranks of actual party leaders, because of their influence with public men, their hold upon opinion, and their experience in public business. Their messages were of the first consequence in the guidance of legislation and the formation of opinion out-of-doors; their spokesmen and friends usually spoke for the President's party as well as for the President himself on the floor of Congress. Even then, however, there had been signs of a new order coming in. Neither the President nor the members of his cabinet had had access to the floor of Congress since Mr. Jefferson decided not to meet the houses in person, as his predecessors had done. It was the theory of constitutional lawyers that Congress and the Executive were meant to be sharply separated and distinguished in function, in order that each might check and balance the other in ideal accordance with the principles of M. Montesquieu; and there were often-times men in the houses whose gifts and impulse of initiative were greater, more efficient, more serviceable than the President's. Mr. Clay had been notable among such men. While he was Speaker of the House of Representatives it became evident that the speakership could easily be made the chief place of power in the management of parties; and so long as he remained in Congress the whole country knew that he, and no President the Whigs were likely to elect, must be the real leader of his party.

That General Jackson dictated the policy of the Democrats while he was President all the world perceived; but his successors were not men of his stamp. Affairs, moreover, were presently turned from their normal course by the extraordinary pressure of the slavery question. Upon that perplexing matter, so disputable, so full of heat, apparently so impossible of definitive settlement, always holding a crisis at its heart, parties made no confident stand. Definite leadership seemed out of the question, until Mr. Douglas came and brought a revolution on. All things waited upon the slow movement of moral, social, economic forces, upon the migrations of population, upon the insensible shiftings of sentiment, upon change and circumstance. Not until the war came, with issues which needed no definition at the hands of the politician, with tasks which called, not for debate, but for concentration and energy, did the organization of party power in Congress take the shape it was to keep through the next generation,— the new generation which should conduct the war to its close and then attempt to set the policies of peace afoot again. Then, with Congress purged of the southern Democrats and all organized opposition cleared away, the Republican leaders equipped Congress for effective mastery. The Senate, indeed, kept its leisurely rules, still chose its committees by ballot, and declined to put itself under the whip of rigid party discipline as the House did, which seemed to regard itself as meant to be an administrative, not a deliberative body. The House put itself into the hands of its leaders for action.

Its leaders were the chairmen of its principal standing committees and its Speaker. The Speaker appointed the committees. In determining the membership of those which were to handle the chief matters of its business he could determine also the policy they were to urge upon the House. For the House put itself very absolutely into the hands of its committees. Individual initiative told for little against them.

The first Speaker of the war time, Mr. Galusha Grow, of Pennsylvania, was a man cast for the rôle of leader, quick, aggressive, confident alike in opinion and in purpose, a thorough partisan, and yet honest and open and ready for responsibility, a man who would use the committees for mastery; and Mr. Schuyler Colfax, who succeeded him, in the second Congress of the war time, was equally well qualified to keep the management of the House in hand, his good nature and easy tact being as influential as his confident initiative in keeping legislation to the paths he had marked out. Both men acted in close co-operation with Mr. Stevens and the other chief masters of the majority upon the floor. The conferences of a few men decided always what the composition of committees should be, the course of legislative action, the time and part allotted to debate. The necessity for action was constantly pressing upon Congress throughout those anxious years; no man ventured to stand long in the way of the public business; and by the time the war was over the House had been converted into a most efficient instrument of party rule. Mr. Johnson learned what its mastery was, how spirited, how irresistible; General Grant looked to its leaders for initiative in affairs. The Speaker and the little group of party managers drawn about him for counsel were henceforth to be in no small part the framers of the policy of the government.

The change was for a long time not observed by the

GALUSHA AARON GROW

country at large, because the two parties offset each other in the houses and neither could take entire command of affairs. For fourteen years (1876–1890) neither party during any one session controlled both the houses and the presidency, except for a brief space of two years (1881–1883) when the Republicans, with a Republican President in the chair, had, by the use of the Vice President's casting vote in the Senate, a majority of a single vote in each house. So scant a margin was not a margin of power, and the Speaker happened for the nonce to be of the older type, not cast for leadership.

That long deadlock of the houses was of much more serious consequence than the mere postponement of a full application of the new methods of party leadership and legislative management. So long as it lasted no change could be made in the laws passed in support of Republican supremacy and negro suffrage in the South. The country had turned away from the Republicans, as the elections to the House showed afresh every two years, but the majority of the nation and the majority of the States were by no means one and the same, and the Senate came only for a little while into the hands of the Democrats, while a Republican President was in the chair. Democratic majorities, accordingly, did not avail to repeal the " Force Acts " and the federal law for the supervision of elections which put the southern political leaders in danger of the federal courts and kept men of the President's appointment at the polls in the South to act in behalf of the negroes and the Republican managers. Though the white men of the South were at last in control of their state governments, federal law still held them off from excluding negroes from the exercise of the suffrage by any fair or open method which should set aside without breach of law what reconstruction had done. They were driven, if the incubus of that ignorant and hostile vote was to be lifted from their affairs, to resort to covert, tricky, fraudulent means which brought their own deep demoralization.

Every device known to politicians, every plan that could be hit upon that politicians had never before been driven to resort to, was made use of to reduce or nullify the negro vote. It was a great advantage to the men who had regained their power in the South that the whole machinery of elections, at least, was again in their hands. They had never before made such use of it. The older traditions that surrounded the use of the ballot in the South were of the most honorable sort. But the poison of the reconstruction system had done its work,—no man any longer found it hard to learn methods of mastery which were not the methods of law or honor or fair play. The new election officers found many excuses for rejecting or ignoring the negroes' voting papers. Voting places were often fixed at points so remote from the centres of population that only a small proportion of the negroes could reach them during the hours for voting; or were changed without notice so that only the white voters who had been informed could find them readily. In some cases separate ballot boxes were used for the several offices to be filled at the elections, so lettered that the illiterate negroes distinguished them with difficulty and so shifted in their order from time to time that the sequence in which they stood was constantly being changed, and no vote was counted which was not put into the right box. In districts where the negroes mustered in unusual numbers too few voting places were provided, and the voters were prevented from casting their ballots rapidly by premeditated delays of all sorts, so that the full vote of the district could not be cast.

The southern legislatures hastened to adopt the device long ago originated by Mr. Gerry, of Massachusetts, and so divided the voting districts of the States as to seg-

Elbridge Gerry   ELBRIDGE GERRY

regate the negroes within a few districts, whimsically drawn upon the map in such a way as to seek out and include the regions in which they were chiefly massed. The "shoe-string district" contrived by the law-makers of Mississippi, which ran its devious way across the

State for three hundred miles with a width of but twenty, became known the country over as a type of what was being done to cut the negroes off from political power in the South. Where such shifts and expedients failed of their desired result or could not be made use of actual fraud was practised. The less scrupulous partisans of the white party managers folded tissue ballots within their regular voting papers and overcame the negro majority by multiple voting. Dissuasion, too, and all the less noticeable means of intimidation, played their quiet part the while in keeping the negroes away from the polls, and the negro vote fell off by the thousand. There was presently nothing left of the one-time party organization of the Republicans in the South except that the federal office holders appointed by Republican Presidents still essayed to play an influential part among the negroes, and hold them to their party allegiance.

Slowly cases tried under the various Enforcement Acts which had been meant to secure the negroes against interference and intimidation in the exercise of their civil rights crept up, by appeal, to the Supreme Court of the United States and began one by one to be reached on its interminable docket; and in each case the court declared the powers Congress had assumed in those Acts clearly incompatible with the constitution. The right of the negroes to assemble and to bear arms, for example, which Congress had sought to protect and which southern white men had repeatedly interfered with, was a right which they enjoyed, the court declared, as citizens of the States, not as citizens of the United States, and it was not competent for Congress or the federal courts to punish individuals who interfered with it. The power conferred upon Congress by the Thirteenth, Fourteenth, and Fifteenth Amendments, to secure the negroes equality of civil rights with the whites, was, it decided, a power given to be exercised in restraint of the States, not against individuals, as the Act against the "conspiracies" of the Ku Klux had used it, and the States, not the federal government, must punish those who sought to destroy that equality. The legislation which General Grant had put so energetically into execution was unconstitutional and void. But it was 1882 before that sweeping conclusion was reached; the Acts had been executed long ago and their consequences were complete. Only the thought of constitutional lawyers and the course to be pursued by the federal government for the future were cleared by the belated decisions.

More and more the attention of the country, and even of politicians, was being drawn away from the South to the forces of change which were playing through the whole nation, to the determination alike of policy and of party fortunes. The four years of Mr. Hayes's term in the presidency, with their restful discontinuance of party legislation, afforded not only a time of calm in which thoughtful men could look about them, but also a clear stage upon which it quickly became evident that new scenes were being set. It was significant that the first summer of Mr. Hayes's reign of peace was marked by labor disturbances of a magnitude and difficulty hitherto unknown in America. On the 14th of July, 1877, strikes began among the employees of the Baltimore and Ohio, the Pennsylvania, the Erie, and the New York Central railways, the chief trunk lines between East and West, which for a time assumed almost the proportions of an armed insurrection. Thousands of miners at the coal mines of Pennsylvania left their work along with the railway men, until there were presently, it might be, a hundred thousand men not only idle but bent upon mischief also, determined to hold the business of the railways at a standstill and prevent at all hazards the employment of others in

BLOCKADE OF ENGINES AT MARTINSBURG, VIRGINIA

their places. Not until troops of the United States had been called out to aid the militia of the States was order restored and the property of the railway companies secured against pillage and destruction. Railway traffic had been held still in a sort of paralysis for two long weeks; property whose value was estimated at ten million dollars had been destroyed; and the country had been given a startling demonstration of the power of the labor organizations.

BURNING OF THE ROUND HOUSE AT PITTSBURG, PENNSYLVANIA

Such outbreaks were undoubtedly a sign of the times
and showed very plainly the new, unregulated economic
forces which were in a future near at hand to exercise
a potent influence on politics and the plans of parties.
But they were at least gross, tangible, susceptible of
being handled by counter force and sheer authority.
There were subtler economic forces than these at work,
harder to handle, more to be feared. Ideas were rapidly
gaining ground in the ranks of all parties which seemed
likely, if unchecked, to break party lines athwart in
novel confusion and turn the government away from
some of its oldest, best established lines of policy. They
chiefly concerned the currency. Congress had met
the extraordinary expenses of the war by measures
which had in fact revolutionized the traditional financial policy of the government. Taxes had not yielded

enough, loans could not be had fast enough, and early in 1862 it had begun the issue of notes from the Treasury of the United States which were for the time irredeemable, but which were nevertheless made legal tender in the payment of debts. Late in 1861 (December 28th) the banks of the country had suspended specie payments. The paper of the government became almost the only currency, and its bulk rose steadily from million to million. War and the depreciation of the currency brought in their train an inflation of prices. Farmers had been getting little profit from their crops when the war began. The cost of transporting them to market over the railways had lifted the cost of their production quite to the level of what the merchants would give for them. Many planters used their corn for fuel. But the war made grain exceedingly valuable. The purchases of the government alone changed the whole face of the market. Money was once more easy to get, the paper money of the Treasury, and could be used at its face value as well as gold itself to pay the mortgages off which the older time of stress had piled up. The "greenbacks" of the government became for the agricultural regions of the North and West a symbol of prosperity.

Conservative constitutional lawyers had doubted from the first the legality of these issues. Every serious student of the times in which the constitution had been framed, and of the dominant motives of its framers, was convinced that one of the chief objects of the statesmen who led the convention of 1787 had been to put government in America once for all upon a solid footing of sound financial policy. The constitution explicitly forbade the issue of paper money by the States,

and the right to issue it was not to be found among the
enumerated powers granted to Congress. It was known
to have been intentionally omitted; and in 1869 the Supreme Court had decided that the treasury issues of the
war time were, as legal tender, unconstitutional and
void. For a little while it had looked as if the law of
the constitution was to be made a permanent bar to
financial experiment. But the decision of the court
had been reached by only a single vote, changes in
its *personnel* occurred almost immediately, and in 1870
the decision was reversed. Congress was at liberty to
make what experiments it pleased.

Thoughtful public men saw, nevertheless, that the
business interests of the country rendered it imperative
that by statute, if not by constitutional compulsion,
specie payments should be resumed by the government, the redundant currency of the country contracted,
and money transactions put once more upon foundations that would hold fast. Gold had been made the
single standard of value in the United States by an
Act of Congress passed in 1853. That Act had said
nothing about the silver dollar of the earlier coinage,
because it had in fact passed out of circulation. The
Act of 1873 had simply recognized that fact and dropped the 412½ grain silver dollar from the list of coins.
An Act of January 14, 1875, had provided for the re-
sumption of specie payments by the government on
the 1st of January, 1879. Every promise of the government was on and after that date to be redeemable in
gold. By 1876 an extraordinary fall had taken place
in the value of silver. It had been coming in augmented
quantities from the mines; Germany and even the states
of the Latin Union, associated by treaty for the ex-

press purpose of maintaining a stable ratio between gold and silver in their exchanges, had suspended the coinage of silver; the demand for it had greatly fallen off at the very time that its quantity had increased, and the price of silver bullion fell as it had never fallen before. The real functions of money, the real laws of its value, the real standards of its serviceability, its real relations to trade and to industry have always been hidden from the minds of men whose thought in such matters has not been trained by the actual experiences of the open markets of the world, in actual exchange, or in the actual direction of the financial operations of governments. The coincidence of high prices and eager markets with floods of paper poured from the Treasury of the United States, coupled with the indisputable fact that the return to slacker demand, lower prices, and a greater scarcity of money had been accompanied by a considerable contraction of the redundant currency and by laws which were soon to bring about a return to specie payments, a turning back from "cheap" money to "dear," confused the thinking even of some men who had long been in contact with public affairs; and those who could not go quite the length of the "Greenbackers" turned to silver for relief.

Gold was not abundant enough, they said, to serve as the sole basis of the country's expanding business, get the farmers' crops to market, or settle the varied balances of trade. Silver was both cheaper and more abundant. The obligations of the United States had been made payable "in coin"; why must they be paid in the dearest of coins? Why could they not be paid in the old silver dollar of 412½ grains, until 1873 the undisputed standard silver dollar of the national coinage? It was in part the suggestion of the owners of the silver mines of Colorado and Nevada, no doubt, who had influential spokesmen in Congress; but they alone could have created no determining opinion in the matter. The real force of the sentiment came from the uneasy economic conditions of the country. The farmers found themselves at the mercy of the railways in getting their crops to market; prices had fallen; money was not easy to get as it had happened to be when abundant issues of paper came pouring every month from the government's treasury; the gold which Congress had sought to make the sole basis of the country's business was in the hands of the great eastern bankers; the railways were in the hands of the capitalists of the East, whom the bankers served. If the bankers set themselves against every proposition to provide an irredeemable paper currency again or even a fresh coinage of silver, there was the more reason to believe that paper or silver was the only real " people's " money. The sentiment grew within Congress and without and concentrated itself upon the question of a silver coinage. Reason had not established it and reason could not check or dislodge it. It took hold upon Republicans and Democrats alike, and within a year of Mr. Hayes's accession to the presidency had won majorities in both houses which were large enough to override the President's veto.

Mr. Bland, of Missouri, introduced in the House a bill which provided for the free and unlimited coinage of silver into standard dollars of 412½ grains at the mints of the United States at the pleasure of those who presented silver bullion which they wished so converted. The finance committee of the Senate, under the leadership of Senator Allison, of Iowa, when the bill reached them, substituted for it a measure which provided for the monthly purchase by the Treasury of not less than two million dollars' worth of silver bullion and its coinage into standard silver dollars which should be legal tender, without restriction of amount, in the payment of all debts. The Secretary of the Treasury was authorized at his discretion to expend as much as four millions monthly for the purpose. The House accepted the measure which Mr. Allison's committee had substituted for its own. Mr. Hayes vetoed it, but the houses passed it over his veto, February 28, 1878. The majority for it was as decisive in the Republican Senate as in the Democratic House. Specie payments were resumed on the 1st of

RICHARD P. BLAND

January, 1879, as the Act of 1875 directed, but silver had been added to gold. The Secretary of the Treasury made his purchases of silver bullion at its market value in gold, of course; its price fell in spite of the Bland-Allison Act, because it was governed, as every man of experience in such matters knew it must be, by influences as wide as the markets of the world; and the monthly coinage steadily yielded more than two million

147

coined dollars of the fineness prescribed by Congress, though the Secretary of the Treasury confined himself always to the expenditure of the minimum sum

WILLIAM B. ALLISON

fixed by the Act. Not many of the coined dollars themselves got into the currents of trade. The Act had authorized the Secretary to issue certificates in their place to those who did not wish the actual silver, and the coins steadily accumulated in the vaults of the Treasury, some thirty millions a year.

This was the only legislation of importance, apart from the routine business of the government, that a Republican Senate and a Democratic House could agree upon. All party purposes of necessity stood in abeyance. Mr. Hayes had as little political authority as Mr. Johnson had had. He had been chosen, as Mr. Franklin Pierce had been twenty-five years before, from outside the ranks of the authoritative leaders of his party. He had no real hold upon the country. His amiable character, his lack of party heat, his conciliatory attitude towards the South alienated rather than attracted the members of his party in Congress. They had been accustomed to see the fight forced for coercion and supremacy in the South, as for the execution of every other party purpose, and the zest for strong measures was still upon them. The President, besides, would not listen to them in matters of appointment to office, as General Grant had listened, to his undoing, but went calmly about to have his own way in dispensing the patronage. The Democrats did not like him because he seemed to them incapable of frank, consistent action. He withdrew the troops from the southern States to let politics there take their normal course, and yet he appointed the one-time members of the discredited returning boards to federal offices, as if to console them for their loss of power. He was not aggressive enough to draw a party of his own about him, and yet he had a character too firm, too self-respecting, too deeply touched with a sense of individual responsibility to accept advice which his own judgment did not approve. He went his own course and kept affairs at their quiet

CHESTER ALAN ARTHUR

poise, awaiting a change of weather. The second Congress of his term was Democratic in both branches and made trial of every expedient known to parliamentary strategy to force upon him a repeal of the statutes which gave federal supervisors and marshals powers of oversight and arrest at the southern polls; but the President was too stout a partisan to consent and stood fast against them. All things stood as they were until the elections should come again.

Mr. Hayes was not nominated for a second term. Determined efforts were made in the Republican nominating convention, which met June 5, 1880, at Chicago, to nominate General Grant again and return to the party's old régime; but they were defeated, and Mr. James A. Garfield, of Ohio, was named as the party's new candidate for the presidency, Mr. Chester A. Arthur, of New York, as its candidate for the vice presidency. Neither of the candidates could claim especial eminence. Mr. Garfield had won high rank and enviable distinction as an officer of volunteers in the war, had become a member of the House when the struggle had but just passed its central crisis at Gettysburg, and had served continuously there until chosen a senator of the United States in the very year of his nomination for the presidency, without making himself felt except for his attractive personality, his serviceable confidence and courage as a parliamentary leader, and his power as an orator. But he stood within the intimate counsels of his party as Mr. Hayes did not. Mr. Arthur had been collector of the port of New York, but had stood for the most part aside from national politics, a lawyer and managing servant of his party within the State rather than a conspicuous figure in its general counsels.

WINFIELD SCOTT HANCOCK

They were not men to catch the enthusiasm of the country. But the party that was back of them had gathered again some of its old momentum; the Democrats had no policy to propose which seemed vital or of the new age

WILLIAM H. ENGLISH

that had come in, and presented as their candidates only an attractive soldier, General Winfield Scott Hancock, and Mr. William H. English, a successful business man of Indiana, who had been no politician since Kansas was admitted to the Union. Though the Democratic

153

voters mustered strong at every polling place and fell but a little more than nine thousand behind the Republicans in a total vote of more than nine millions, they carried no States north of Mason and Dixon's line except New Jersey, Maryland, California, and Nevada, and Mr. Garfield was chosen President by a majority of fifty-nine in the electoral college (214–155).

The only note of new questions sounded in the campaign came from the convention of the "Greenback-Labor Party," in which reformers of the more radical sort had united. It had declared, turning to what seemed for the moment the chief question of the day, that "all money, whether metallic or paper, should be issued and its volume controlled by the government, and not by or through banking corporations, and, when so issued, should be full legal tender for all debts, public and private." It had demanded that the greenback notes of the war time "should be substituted for the notes of the national banks, the national banking system abolished, and the unlimited coinage of silver, as well as gold, established by law." But for the present the country preferred to make choice, not among new parties, but between the old, which it knew, and the programme of the new party got but a few more than three hundred thousand votes out of the nine millions cast. The Democrats not only failed to get the presidency but also lost their majorities both in the House and in the Senate, though by a margin so slender that the Republicans were to find that they could make little confident or aggressive use of their advantage.

The transition from Mr. Hayes to Mr. Garfield seemed but a natural exchange of a man who did not lead for a man who had a real hold on the affections and the

J. A. Garfield

JAMES ABRAM GARFIELD

allegiance of his party and could stand at its front to make policy; but it had scarcely been made when the air seemed to fill with ominous signs of sinister disquiet. The poisonous influences which had long been gathering about the system of appointments to office, the spirit of intrigue and of personal aggrandizement, the insistent scheming and dictation of members of the houses to force their preferences and the arguments of their private interest upon the acceptance of the President, the brazen, indecent clamor of the meaner sort of partisans for preferment, seemed of a sudden to work with fatal violence upon affairs. Mr. Garfield asserted a will of his own in the matter, and the two senators from New York, Mr. Roscoe Conkling and Mr. Thomas Collier Platt, resigned their seats, as if upon some weighty quarrel in matters of state, because he would not heed their wishes and choose their nominee in naming a collector for the port of New York. Office seekers swarmed about the President with quite unwonted arrogance, and before he had been four months in his uneasy place of authority one of the crowding throng whom he had disappointed wreaked foul vengeance upon him. On the morning of the 2d of July, 1881, as he passed through a railway station at Washington on his way to the seaside to seek a much needed respite from the harassments of those first months of bitter wrangle and discord, he was shot by Charles Jules Guiteau, a man maddened by disappointed vanity because he had not obtained the office he sought. For eighty days the President lingered between life and death, but death conquered, and on the 19th of September the end came. On the 20th Mr. Arthur took the oath as President.

Thoughtful men had looked about them, the while, to see what this new and sinister thing meant. Some part of its explanation lay upon the surface. It might, no doubt, fairly be ascribed, in part at least, to the sharp factional split that had shown itself in the Republican

THOMAS COLLIER PLATT

ranks in the convention which had nominated Mr. Garfield. The "stalwarts" of the party, whom Mr. Conkling had led, and who had fought desperately in the convention to secure the renomination of General Grant, were of the older temper of the party, had hated Mr. Hayes very cordially for his mildness and lack of partisan vigor, and were bent upon carrying Republicans back to the methods which others saw had discredited them in their day of power. They had been defeated by the "halfbreeds" of the convention, as they contemptuously designated their opponents within the party, and Mr. Garfield was in their eyes the representative of the halfbreeds. Mr. Conkling had supported him in the campaign, despite his feeling of personal defeat, and Mr. Conkling's friends felt sure that his eloquence and personal influence had availed as nothing else could have availed to keep the State of New York to its allegiance to the Republicans in the election. His generosity in that matter they deemed worthy of reward. But Mr. Garfield would yield him no special consideration; and, because the President held himself resolutely at a balance as between faction and faction in his use of the patronage and pointedly ignored the wish of the stalwarts in his appointment to the collectorship of the port of New York, Mr. Conkling had flung out of the Senate and appealed to the legislature of New York for re-election, as a demonstration of power against the President. He had failed. The legislature would not so rebuke the President. But factional bitterness had been wrought to the highest pitch, and the tragedy of the President's death seemed to the country an object lesson in its consequences.

The attention of the country was fixed at last, with painful intensity of interest, upon the character and influence of the civil service. Not a little of the true nature of the existing system of appointments to office had been laid bare by Mr. Conkling's extraordinary act of self-assertion. The use of appointments as rewards for party services did not, it seemed, bind partisans together, after all, as the advocates of the spoils system claimed, or compact and discipline parties for aggressive and successful action. Worked out through its detail of local bosses, senatorial and congressional "influence," personal favors, the placating of enemies and the full satisfaction of friends, it must always men-

CHARLES JULES GUITEAU

ace the successful party itself with factional disruption. Guiteau, the assassin, had said that he fired his shots for the "stalwarts," that Mr. Arthur, their friend, might be President; and those murderous shots still rang in the ear of the country like a startling confirmation of all that the advocates of civil service reform had said. Congressmen saw opinion at last set steadily, irresistibly

159

towards radical measures of reformation, with a force and certainty it had never shown before, and Democrats and Republicans found one more question upon which, opinion beating upon them as it did, they must agree. In August, 1881, while the President lay dying, various local associations which had been formed to agitate the question of the reform of the civil service were drawn together, in a meeting held at Newport, Rhode Island, into a National Civil Service Reform League, whose first act was to express its hearty approbation of a bill for the reform of the service which Mr. Pendleton, of Ohio, had introduced the preceding year in the Senate.

The bill would no doubt have lain almost unnoticed on the docket of the Senate had not Mr. Conkling's arrogance and Guiteau's madness of bitter passion disposed all the country to consider what must be done. Mr. Pendleton was a Democrat, but he spoke only for himself and for other men of like conviction in the matter, not for his party, in the bill in which he proposed a return to the system of competitive appointments which Congress had authorized in 1872 and abandoned in 1874. Neither did he speak for the party in power, who regarded such a measure as a mere curtailment of its political influence. Even the tragedy of 1881 did not shake the politicians from their stubborn hostility. For almost two years the bill lingered and made no progress, despite the unmistakable evidences of opinion out-of-doors. But the elections of 1882 sufficed to bring it to life. In the Congress chosen in 1880 the Republicans predominated, by a bare majority, too small to use, in both houses. But the elections of 1882 put into the House a Democratic majority of more than eighty and aroused the Republicans to a sudden sense of their responsibility to the public opinion of the country. The Senate, changing by States, not by the sweep of the popular vote, remained in their hands; their ma-

ROSCOE CONKLING

jority there was even increased. In the existing Senate they had had to rely on the casting vote of the Vice President for their majority; in the new Senate they were to command a serviceable majority of four. But they read the signs of the weather with as keen an apprehension as if they had lost both Senate and House. The Democrats, on their part, were ready to enhance their growing credit with the country by showing themselves willing advocates of reform. On the 6th of January, 1883, accordingly, before the new Congress met, the Pendleton bill passed both houses by large majorities, almost as if without serious dissent; and Mr. Arthur signed it at once with hearty approval.

It provided for appointments to office by competitive examination and for the constitution of a Civil Service Commission which should be charged with the execution of its provisions, the establishment of proper tests, the conduct of examinations, and the careful enforcement of the rules of eligibility. It did not include all classes of the civil service, but it at least took rank and file, all clerical offices and all offices not of special trust and confidence, out of the reach of the politicians, and began a reform which the President could, under the terms of the Act itself, extend at his pleasure. Mr. Arthur sought to have it administered efficiently and in thorough good faith, for it had his sincere approval. He had shown from the first a dignity, a tact, a firmness, a sense of public duty in the administration of the great office so unexpectedly thrust upon him which had filled the country not less with surprise than with deep satisfaction. His selection by the Republicans for the vice presidency had given even stout partisans uncomfortable misgivings. He had been known in New York as of the group of office-holding politicians rather than as a man devoted to the larger kind of public service; his company had been that of the petty managers of the party's local interests, more interested in patronage than in public questions, a "stalwart" who took his cue from larger men. But the presidency brought his finer qualities to light. His messages and state papers read like the productions of a man of unusual capacity, information, and literary power. He seemed to make his chief appointments with a view to the efficiency of the public service rather than with a view to political advantage. He dealt with the bills sent to him by Congress in a way that lacked neither courage nor discrimination. Faction was quieted and the course of affairs ran cool again, with an air in which men could think.

There was need for dispassionate thinking. Each year disclosed more clearly than the year which had preceded it the altered temper of the times, the questions of industrial development, of the relations between capital and labor, of tariff readjustment, and of currency reform which must take precedence of the older questions of politics, of constitutional privilege and civil rights, which had cut the former lines of cleavage between parties. The tariff duties which had been adjusted to the conditions and financial necessities of the war time were now piling up in the Treasury balances too large to be used. Obviously something must be done to ease the country of the unnecessary burden. Democrats and Republicans could not easily agree upon such a question. It was an old question in a new guise and had always separated Democrats from the Whigs from whom Republicans took their traditions in such a matter. The first approaches to reform were made very slowly, therefore, very guardedly, with a handsome show of careful consideration but very little show of action. In the winter of 1881–1882 a commission was appointed to travel through the country and take testimony with regard no less to the local than to the national conditions of trade and industry, for the purpose of supplying Congress with trustworthy data upon which to act in reducing the duties. Its report was in due course made, and an Act was passed which effected a reduction of duties which was in substantial accord with its recommendations. But the majority of the commission had been made up of stout protectionists, and the changes in the tariff which it recommended made little difference either in the revenues or in the incidence of taxation.

It began to be plainly evident, moreover, that the tariff question was but a part of that general question of the development of trade and industry which year by year grew so various, so complex, so difficult to set justly apart in its elements. The country was undoubtedly prosperous. The South, especially, was showing how it could respond to the economic stimulation of the time, to the general development of the resources of the country, now that its corrupt governments, with their negro majorities, were lifted from its shoulders. But the very expansion of industry, the very growth and cumulative productiveness of capital made difficulties of their own,—difficulties novel, unlooked for, in the handling of which statesmen were without experience or precedent and even men of business without standards of judgment. Capitalists were effecting a novel concentration of their power, through corporate association, through united lines of railway, through extensive combinations in industrial undertakings which created a sort of league to control both the output and the prices. And laborers, finding that they had to deal no longer with individual employers, but with powerful groups of men whom they never

AN OBSERVATION CAR ON THE PACIFIC RAILROAD

saw and could speak with only through their agents, themselves drew together in leagues, larger than the old trades unions, in order that workingmen as well as employers might wield the power of wide combination. Even laborers of different occupations drew together. So long ago as 1869 a society had been formed in Philadelphia, upon the initiative of a sagacious tailor, one Uriah Stevens, to unite workingmen of different occupations for their mutual benefit and protection, not only in respect of their relations with their employers, but also in respect of their relations with one another and the general advancement of their interests. Before statesmen saw what new questions were before them it had grown into a " Noble Order of Knights of Labor," whose membership was numbered in figures which exceeded one hundred thousand. A new economic force had come upon the field.

Financial disaster, a time of sharp stringency when men looked to their investments, regretted their loans, questioned every adventure of business, and stood dismayed to see the prosperity of the country of a sudden checked, it might be destroyed, added its thrill of excitement and of apprehension to bring the thought of the country to an imperative reckoning upon economic questions. As in 1873, so again now it was the too rapid development of railways, their too desperate competition for earnings which were at best insufficient to support them, and the reckless speculation of those who dealt in their stocks that brought the sudden contraction of values on, and then panic and ruin. The country was growing very rapidly alike in population and in the increase of wealth and the multiplication of resources. The census taken in 1880 had shown that the population had, within the preceding ten years, increased more than thirty *per cent.*, from 38,558,371 to 50,155,783. It was estimated that the actual wealth of the country had within the same period increased quite forty-five *per cent.*, from $30,068,518,507 to $43,-642,000,000. Nothing had lagged. Agriculture, manufactures, commerce, the products of the mines and of every industry that added to the resources of the country and made it rich and quick with energy showed a sound and wholesome growth commensurate with crowding numbers and the zest of hopeful enterprise. But the construction of railways had outrun all reason in the attempt to keep pace with the country's growth. The total railway mileage of the United States had been increased from 52,914 to 93,671 within the decade. New lines had bid against the old for patronage by sharp reductions in the rates of carriage; rates had fallen below the actual cost of the service; and while ruinous competition cut away profits, speculation in railway securities in the stock market completed the mischief. That speculation had reached its highest point of reckless adventure in 1880. After that the prices of railway securities began to decline, at first only a little, then very sharply, and in May, 1884, the inevitable crash came. As usual, some firms upon the Street suffered not only ruin but dishonor also, among the rest the firm of Grant and Ward, in which General Grant had been a silent partner. He had known nothing of the dishonorable transactions of his partners, but the disgrace and ruin in which they involved him touched his last days with humiliation and with a deep sadness which he could not shake off. Unscrupulous men had played upon him in business as they had played upon him in politics, and men's minds went always backwards to find his time of glory.

Financial crisis did not, of course, touch the real resources of the country; its business went forward without fatal embarrassment, and those who took the large view of affairs perceived that its prosperity was not in fact seriously checked by what had happened in Wall Street. But Wall Street was, none the less, the seat of credit, and acute disturbances in its market could not go by without consequences which all the country felt. Business could not, for a little while, move with as confident a spirit as before. It was evident, too, that in undertakings both great and small the friction between laborers and employers grew, not less, but greater, as if some unwholesome influence were at work to clog the productive processes of the time. Workingmen promptly adapted to their own use against employers the "boycott" which Irish agitators had originated to work the ruin of those who opposed their radical programmes of social and political reform or who stood out for the privileges of the hated land owners. Individuals or companies who would not yield to the dictation of the labor organizations in any matter, whether of employment, wages, or hours of work, they sought to cut off from all patronage and business by terrorizing all who dealt with them or approached their places of business; and the courts were forced to execute, sometimes very harshly, the law against conspiracy, fitting formulas originated in an age gone by to circumstances more difficult to form their judgments upon than any a past age had produced. It added a little, too, to the sense of disquietude created by the crisis in the money market and the chronic disorders of in-

dustry that unprecedented and disastrous floods occurred, in the summer of 1884, in the valley of the Ohio,
breeding distresses and tumults in the city of Cincinnati
which put the place for six days together almost at
the mercy of mobs.

The country got from every quarter a disquieting
sense of lax government, deranged business, bad
management in affairs, and the dissatisfaction and
anxiety which such impressions produced inevitably
operated to discredit the party in power. Some radical
change in leadership began to seem desirable. Opinion
more and more wearied of the stale grounds of preference
upon which parties and candidates were chosen at the
polls. The Republicans had held the presidency ever
since the war, and both houses of Congress until 1875,
not because they met new questions with new policy,
but because, in a day now gone by, they had been the
party of the Union and had saved it. Tenure of power
through a whole generation, as if by prescriptive right,
had worked its own demoralization, as was inevitable
among men who made no new plans and had no new
impulse of reform. Mr. Hayes had been upright, public
spirited, inclined to serve the country unselfishly and
in the interest of sound policy; Mr. Arthur had come
out of the unpromising ranks of office holders and local
party managers and yet had shown himself a man of
elevated ideals in administration; but observant lookers
on got the impression, none the less, that the lax morals
and questionable practices of General Grant's day
were still to be found beneath the surface of the public
business at Washington. Men everywhere believed
that the fibre of the party in power was relaxed and
that new blood must somehow be got into the govern-

ment before it could be made secure against the bad
methods and the vicious standards of action which
had got possession of it. It was not an issue as between parties that was shaping itself in the public mind,
but rather a desire to choose new men, whichever party
should prove ready to supply them,—the newer, the
less identified with the party policies of the generation
then passing away, the better. Upon that desire the
presidential campaign of 1884 turned. Had the Republicans named a man of such qualities as to make
the country feel sure of him as an instrument of integrity and sensible rectification in public affairs, no doubt
he would have been chosen President; but they did
not name such a man. The Democrats did, and won.
Mr. Grover Cleveland, whom the Democratic convention put forward, was a new man in the field of national
politics, but had proved his quality in public service
in the State of New York in a way which had, within
the past two or three years, attracted the attention of
the whole country. Twenty years before, when he was
but a youth of twenty-six, he had been chosen district
attorney for the city of Buffalo (1863); in 1871 he had
been made sheriff of his county, and ten years later
mayor of Buffalo; in 1882 he became governor of the
State. In that year the tide of popular reaction against
the Republicans had run very strong, and Pennsylvania
and Massachusetts, as well as New York, had preferred
Democratic to Republican governors; but the reaction
had been more marked and extraordinary in New York
than anywhere else. In 1880, the year Mr. Garfield
was chosen President, the Republicans had carried
New York by a safe margin of more than 21,000 votes;
and yet in 1882, but two years later, Mr. Cleveland had

been preferred to an unimpeachable opponent by a plurality of 190,000.

He was of the open and downright sort that all men who love strength must always relish. Business men felt that they could trust him because he had had business of his own to manage as a lawyer of assured and increasing practice and knew the business interests of the State and meant to guard them. Plain men instinctively trusted him, because they felt sure that they understood him, seeing that he was no subtile politician but a man without sophistication like themselves. He had early been drawn into politics and had followed it with a wholesome relish, finding zest in its comradeships with men of action and resource, men of quick wits and ready expedients, as well as in the sense of action and of service which it brought into his own life. A long apprenticeship in affairs, with local politicians for associates and fellow counsellors, made it very clear to him how men were to be handled and combined and gave him that close acquaintance with the personal side of party combination which is the surest basis of political sagacity among those who lead; and yet, though he knew men of all sorts intimately and at first hand, as Lincoln did, and met them every day in close, sympathetic association, he kept his own principles and point of view unconfused. He was the son of a rural pastor. His father had not had the means to give him a college training, but the lad had got the better training of a Christian household, had brought away from his quiet home standards of right action and a steadfast, candid conscience which told more and more upon the courses of his life as he matured. His associates found candor and courage to

171

be the most characteristic qualities of the man. There was something very satisfactory in the simplicity and frankness with which he went about his duties when in office, without question as to his obligations as a public servant or misgivings as to the effect of what he did upon his personal fortunes. "The affairs of the city," he said, when he became mayor, " should be conducted as far as possible upon the same principle as a good business man manages his private concerns"; and the voters of the city found, with not a little satisfaction, that he acted upon that principle with extraordinary watchfulness and vigor. They dubbed him the "veto mayor" before his term was out, so frequently did he check the extravagance and the ill considered plans of the city council with his sharp, unhesitating executive negative. As governor the same qualities shone even more conspicuous in him. Courage, directness, good sense, public spirit, as if without thought of consequences either to himself or to his party, made him at once a man whom all the country marked when he came to that great post.

There were men in the Republican ranks in New York who had played the chief parts of protest against the tendencies of their party. They meant to reform it, if they could, and so save it, but to oppose it if they could not bring it to a new way of action, a new and better choice of leaders. They sent strong spokesmen to the Republican nominating convention of 1884, and when that convention would not heed them they urged the Democrats to nominate Mr. Cleveland and give independent voters a chance to cast their ballots for a man of their own temper and principles in affairs. The Democratic convention took their advice, and for

JAMES GILLESPIE BLAINE

the first time in twenty-eight years a Democrat was chosen President. The candidate whom the Republicans had preferred was as brilliant a leader as any party had had for a generation; but the country did not want brilliant leadership; it wished for mere solidity of character and for a new and better point of view in the man it should put into its highest office; and it could not satisfy itself with Mr. Blaine. Mr. James G. Blaine was a man turned of fifty-four; Mr. Cleveland was but forty-seven. The one had been known through a whole generation as a man who by sheer force of natural gifts, eloquence, audacity, charm, had made his way to the front in the national counsels; the other had come but yesterday into view, not as a leader in counsel, but as a man of right action in practical public business. But some deeply unpleasant impressions had got abroad concerning Mr. Blaine, and had worked very powerfully upon those who were beyond the reach of his personal charm; and when the Republicans nominated him for the presidency the distrust those impressions had bred cost him the election, with such a man as Mr. Cleveland for opponent. He had played a great part in legislation. Three successive times before they lost control of the House of Representatives (1869–1875) the Republicans had made him Speaker, and he had used the power of that great office to make himself master of party action in the lower house, after the manner of the later Speakers, but with a personal hold upon the members of the House such as no man had enjoyed since Henry Clay. There were rumors that he had used his power also to obtain favors from certain railway and mining corporations and enrich himself. Nothing was proved. When the charges made against him were looked into with careful and impartial scrutiny they turned out to have very disputable foundation. He had engaged in transactions which no doubt left his hands clean, but hardly, it seemed, his conscience. There had been too little of the high punctilio of a nice sense of honor in many of the things he had done. Republicans who had grown critical and uneasy in such matters were convinced that, whatever might be said in defence or justification of Mr. Blaine, he was, at best, not entirely free from the taint that had seemed to fall upon almost every leader of the party who had played a prominent part in Congress during the last, bad days of the period of reconstruction, when the power they wielded was touched with high-handed lawlessness and the government they administered with the spirit of spoilsmen.

The result of the election turned upon the vote of New York. No strong tide of popular preference ran for the Democrats such as had heartened them in 1882. Every northern and western State except Connecticut, New Jersey, Indiana, and New York cast its votes for Mr. Blaine; could he have carried New York, he would have been elected, and he lost it by only the very narrow margin of 1,149 votes. In the thought of the New York voters it was one thing to vote for a governor, quite another to vote for a President. The national prestige of the Republican party was not lost; only the steadfast determination of a few men to rid it, if they could, of its older leaders gave the vote of the State to Mr. Cleveland. Their task called for not a little moral courage in the performance. They were in principle and by preference, not Democrats, but Republicans, and what they were about to do filled their one-time party associates with contempt and bitter resentment. They were dubbed pharisees, who must needs prove themselves a saving and holy remnant, truer than their fellows; "mugwumps," big chiefs, who would not take their cue from common men but must signalize their valor apart. They accepted the name "mugwump" very cheerfully. It was a name whimsically borrowed from the language of the Algonquin Indians, was native American, accordingly, and had no sting that they flinched under either in its first or in its ironical meaning. They were led by men who cared little what names they were called by if only they satisfied their principles in what they did: men like Mr. Carl Schurz, who had led the revolt of the Republicans of Missouri twelve years before; men like Mr. George William Curtis, as much statesman and orator as man of letters, with whom politics was not a game of power but a career of duty. It was the good fortune of such men that there were others in goodly numbers who were as indifferent as themselves what jibes were uttered against them provided they won and kept their character in the fight they had entered upon. And they did win. No doubt the Mugwumps made Mr. Cleveland President. He was a man of the sort they most desired, not touched with the older sophistications of politics, his face set forward, his gifts the gifts of right action. They trusted him and believed that he would purify the civil service and bring in a new day in which parties should concentrate their purposes on practical questions of the present.

Mr. Cleveland's task as President was both delicate and difficult. He did not come into power supported by the warm enthusiasm of a people, as General Jackson had come, though no one doubted that he was the people's, not a party's, President. His popular majority over Mr. Blaine was but 23,000. Three hundred and twenty-five thousand votes had been cast for the candidates of the Greenback and the Prohibitionist parties, to which many men had turned for the nonce because they could not bring themselves to vote for Mr. Blaine and would not vote for a candidate of the Democrats, and in their extremity what to do threw their votes away. Out of a total popular vote of more than ten millions, therefore, Mr. Cleveland had lacked an absolute majority by more than three hundred thousand. The congressional elections had given the Democrats a strong working majority again in the House, but the Senate was still Republican. And yet the new President's party wished and expected him to recast the administration of the government in its behoof, as if it were already in its ascendency, and the Mugwumps bade him disregard party, put partisan considerations aside in his appointments to office, and make the government at Washington, as he had made the government at Albany, a sound instrument of public business. It was inevitable that he should disappoint both his party and the leaders of the independents. Fortunately he knew his own mind and was not rendered timid by the difficulties of his task. He accounted himself, not an independent, but a Democrat. His allegiance to his party was of the staunch and loyal sort. He thoroughly believed in its principles and held himself bound to serve it in every legitimate way compatible with the public service. He was a sincere believer in the reform of the civil service which the Mugwumps made so prominent a part of their creed and programme; but he thought it no breach of the principles of that reform to refuse

v.—12   177

reappointment to Republican officials whose statutory term of four years had expired and to put Democrats in their places, to ask for the resignation of Republican officials whose offices brought them into relations of confidence with the administration, or to dismiss those out of the rank and file who showed themselves disposed to use their offices for partisan purposes. He thought it right and wholesome and an act of sound policy to change a civil service which was exclusively Republican in every rank, and which had been exclusively Republican throughout a whole generation, a service in which Democrats had been virtually proscribed, into a service mixed of men of both parties, and a clear matter of traditional right to put Democrats in every chief post of trust.

The thorough-going politicians of the Democratic party were disappointed to the pitch of dismay to find that Mr. Cleveland meant to make no clean sweep of the offices and set his face like flint against the doctrine that appointments to office were the spoils of victory in a presidential contest. Thorough-going reformers were equally disappointed to find that he did not intend to adopt their principles with their own uncompromising austerity. "They are to be treated with respect," Mr. Blaine had written to Mr. Garfield of the reformers, in 1880, "but they are the worst possible political advisers, . . . foolish, vain, without knowledge of measures, ignorant of men, . . . pharisaical, but not practical; ambitious, but not wise; pretentious, but not powerful." Mr. Cleveland knew too much of the sterling character and wide experience of the particular group of reformers who had made his election possible to utter so superficial a judgment about them, or to feel any-

thing but the profoundest respect for their motives
and for their sagacity as men of action. He stood
very near them in his own hopes and purposes, and
felt no touch of Mr. Blaine's resentful contempt for
them. But he was a practical man of affairs and knew
better than they did both the limitations and the theoretical weakness of their programmes. They stood outside the public service as critics; dealt with principles,
not with men; were serviceable in the formation of
opinion, but not in the conduct of government. The
conduct of government they still left to professional
politicians and to men who made public life their
constant object, as they themselves did not; and Mr.
Cleveland understood the public men whom they condemned more justly than they did,—understood them
by reason of lifelong association with them, and knew
that their qualities were better, their gifts a great deal
more serviceable than men who had no dealings with
them supposed them to be. Those who came into direct conference with him and learned to know at first
hand his principles of action found nothing so strong,
so imperative in Mr. Cleveland as his sense of justice,
his sense of right and of fair dealing. He had, they
found, a big conscience open to the airs of all the various world, approachable by all sorts of men, whether
of thought or of affairs. He felt as much bound to
meet the reasonable expectations of the right-minded
politicians of his party as to come up to the require-
ments of the reformers. He knew the practice of party
government as his critics did not, and felt at liberty
to act upon the immemorial understandings of government in that kind wherever he could do so and yet
not violate principles of sound administration. He

meant to use the principles of the civil service reformers for the purpose of making the government pure and
efficient, but not for the purpose of taking it out of the
hands of parties as an instrument of policy. It was
a reform which he perceived could not be brought on
upon a sudden impulse, but must be worked out through
the processes of politics as they stood.

It was his conduct of administration and his attitude
towards Congress rather than large questions of policy
or of party management that held the attention of the
country throughout the four years of his term. The
House kept its Democratic, the Senate its Republican
majority, and party legislation was still out of the question. All energy and initiative seemed for the time
summed up in the President. His quality was as unmistakable as General Jackson's, and yet he had none
of General Jackson's blind impetuosity or mere wilfulness. His individuality was the more marked because
he stood apart from the houses as a power set to check
and criticise them. He had never been a member of a
legislative body. From first to last his experience in
public service had been that of an executive officer.
He held very literally, therefore, to the theory that Congress and the President were not so much associated
as offset in the structure of the government, and was
inclined to be a strict doctrinaire in the exercise of
a complete independence of congressional suggestion.
What most attracted the attention of the country, aside
from his action in the matter of appointments to office,
was the extraordinary number of his vetoes. Most of
them were uttered against pension bills great and
small. Both Democratic House and Republican Senate
were inclined to grant any man or class of men who

had served in the federal armies during the civil war the right to be supported out of the national Treasury, and Mr. Cleveland set himself very resolutely to check their extravagance. He deemed it enough that those who had been actually disabled should receive pensions from the government, and regarded additional gifts, for mere service, both an unjustifiable use of the public money and a gross abuse of charity. When the Senate sought to revive against him the principles of the Tenure of Office Act, which had been passed to thwart Mr. Johnson but suffered to lie forgotten so long as Republicans were in the presidency, and inquired into his reasons for certain removals from office, he met it with an assertion of his constitutional rights as Executive as imperative as General Jackson would have uttered, and put that matter once for all at rest. Both houses learned to respect his intelligence, his conscience, his unhesitating will with a touch of fear such as they had felt towards no other President they could remember.

The new tenor of reform and of individual responsibility he had brought into affairs seemed in some measure to touch Congress also and to dispose it to apply itself to important matters of business which had too long waited to be dealt with, and which could be handled without partisan heat. The most important of these was the establishment of a fixed order of succession to the presidency, in case of the death or disability of both the President and the Vice President. A bill amending the law in that matter had been formulated in the Senate as long ago as the summer of 1882, and since that time had twice been adopted by the Senate; but the House had failed to concur. As the law stood the succession fell to the president *pro tempore* of the

Senate or, if he could not act, to the Speaker of the House of Representatives. But there were times, falling between the sessions of a Congress whose term had expired and the sessions of the Congress chosen to succeed it, when there was neither a president *pro tempore* of the Senate nor a Speaker of the House. There had been such a season while Mr. Arthur was President. There had been an anxious summer when, had death or serious disability overtaken him, there would have been no one to take up the duties of the chief office of the nation. Another season of the same sort came during the very first year of Mr. Cleveland's presidency. Mr. Hendricks, who had been chosen Vice President with Mr. Cleveland, died in November, 1885, and there was a brief interval during which there was no one between the President and a legal lapse of the presidential functions. At its first session, therefore, the Congress which had been chosen at the time of Mr. Cleveland's election passed an Act which placed the heads of the executive Departments in the line of succession, in the order of the creation of their several offices, should they possess the qualifications of age and of birth within the United States prescribed by the constitution in respect of the President and Vice President: the Secretary of State, the Secretary of the Treasury, the Secretary of War, the Attorney General, the Postmaster General, the Secretary of the Navy, the Secretary of the Interior, the Secretary of Agriculture (January 18, 1886); and a matter of much anxiety was happily settled.

The leaders of the two parties were at last ready also to agree upon a final settlement of the mode of counting the electoral votes. It was manifestly imperative that

the recurrence of such a situation as had been brought
about in 1876 by the double electoral returns from South

T. A. Hendricks THOMAS ANDREWS HENDRICKS

Carolina, Florida, and Louisiana should be prevented
by some provision of law which should determine once
for all whence the authoritative and final decision should
emanate as to the validity of disputed votes, but not

183

until now had the heat of that contest been sufficiently dispelled to enable politicians to come to an agreement in the matter. An Act became law on the 3d of February, 1887, which provided that the decision should rest with the States themselves from which the votes came, and Congress should undertake to judge of matter in dispute only when there was in any State such a conflict between two tribunals of appeal as made it necessary that some outside authority should intervene. In such a case the decision of the houses should be reached by concurrent resolution. It took much debate and many conferences to frame the law to the satisfaction of both houses; but it was felt at last that agreement was necessary, and all sensible men hailed the result with gratification.

There were questions also of business and of economic relief which the houses found it possible to agree upon before Mr. Cleveland's term was out. By an Act of the 4th of February, 1887, known as the Interstate Commerce Act, railway corporations operating lines which passed from one State to another were forbidden to make discriminations in their rates as between different shippers or to enter into any combination with competing companies for the purpose of sharing earnings or of "pooling" freight receipts in a common fund to be proportionally divided; and a commission of five persons, to be appointed by the President, was constituted which was given very extensive judicial and mandatory powers for the enforcement of the Act. In the following year an Act was passed which excluded Chinese immigrants from the United States. The Interstate Commerce Act had been introduced by Senator Reagan, of Texas, so long ago as 1884, and had been pressed for three years before obtaining majorities in both houses. Its advocates spoke in the interest of the farmers and of all small shippers,—of all who had felt the power of the railways a burden upon them. It was not disputed that the railway companies had granted lower rates of carriage to the greater manufacturers and producers whose shipments were large, or that they had favored one section of the country at the expense of another; and it was manifest that their discriminations had fallen very heavily upon small farmers and men in the smaller ways of trade and manufacture. There was decided satisfaction throughout the country, therefore, that steps had at last been taken to protect the rank and file. The law which excluded Chinese immigrants had been passed at the urgent solicitation of the men of the Pacific coast. Chinese laborers had poured in there, first by hundreds, then by thousands, finally by hundreds of thousands, until the labor situation of the whole coast had become one almost of revolution. Caucasian laborers could not compete with the Chinese, could not live upon a handful of rice and work for a pittance, and found themselves being steadily crowded out from occupation after occupation by the thrifty, skilful Orientals, who, with their yellow skin and strange, debasing habits of life, seemed to them hardly fellow men at all, but evil spirits, rather. For years together the laborers of the coast and all who wished to aid them had demanded of Congress the exclusion of the Chinese. Failing of aid from that quarter, riot had become their almost habitual means of agitation and self-defence,— riot which sometimes went the awful length of wholesale slaughter in wanton attacks upon the Chinese quarters of the towns. San Francisco had found the matter a veritable menace to government itself. Congress had passed an exclusion bill in 1879, but Mr. Hayes had vetoed it. Negotiation with China had been tried, but she had refused to agree to the exclusion of her people by her own act and consent; and an end was at last made of the matter by the Act of 1888.

Such Acts were but the first fruits of radical economic changes and the rapid developments of trade, industry, and transportation. The laborers and men whom great combinations of capital were in danger of crushing or driving to the wall were making themselves more and more heard and heeded in the field of legislation. The Knights of Labor, who but the other day had numbered only a few more than a hundred thousand, now mustered six hundred thousand strong. What was more significant, airs, not of agitation merely, but of anarchy also were beginning to stir, in a country which until now had been known and envied the world over as a land in which men reverenced "the laws themselves had made," acted under government as under their own self-control, and kept opinion always within the paths of peace. The cities were filling up with foreigners of the sort the Know Nothings had feared; men who had left their homes dissatisfied not merely with the governments they had lived under but with society itself, and who had come to America to speak treasons elsewhere forbidden. For many a long year their incendiary talk had fallen without effect upon the ears of working-men in America, and politicians had been wont to boast that men born in America and men trained in America's school of labor and politics would never listen to it. But the air of the industrial regions of the country had sensibly thickened with the vapors of unwholesome opinion in these last years of unlooked for concentrations of capital and unparalleled growths of corporate power. They still showed themselves most in cities where discontented men and women out of the proletariat of European countries most congregated. The country had startling evidence of the strength and audacity of the anarchist leaders in a great meeting held in May, 1886, in the Haymarket at Chicago, which seemed part of a concerted plan not only to preach but also to practise defiance of law, and which ended in the most serious conflict with the police an American city had ever witnessed. But the infection was spreading outside the cities, too. It began to be seen, when once the matter was laid bare, that men of American training, as well as foreigners, had begun to take the taint of anarchistic sentiment. Even the Knights of Labor were touched with it, despite the conservative influence of their leaders, and nothing but the sharp reaction of opinion caused by the Chicago riot, the country through, checked its quiet spread. Vast organizations like that of the Knights of Labor held loosely together at best; anarchism is the negation of organization; and in proportion as it became anarchistic the great order suffered disintegration and decay. A new order, the American Federation of Labor, sprang up to take its place, and the scene changed very rapidly as one agitation succeeded another. But no one could say that the scene grew more quiet or gave hopeful signs of peace as it shifted.

To Mr. Cleveland it had become evident that not a little of the economic trouble of the time had its root and source in the operation of the tariff. There, it

THE ANARCHIST RIOT IN CHICAGO, ILLINOIS. A DYNAMITE BOMB EXPLODING AMONG THE POLICE

seemed to him, lay the foundations of those economic preferences of one set of men or one section of the country over another which were so deeply irritating the farmers of the South and West, the laborers of the cities and of the centres of manufacture, and the advocates of free competition. Protective tariffs deliberately extended the favors of the government to particular undertakings; only those who had the capital to take advantage of those favors got rich by them; the rest of the country was obliged to pay the costs in high prices and restricted competition. Such had time out of mind been Democratic doctrine, and every sign of the times seemed a demonstration of its truth. But not every man who called himself a Democrat accepted that creed. The Democratic party had been out of power for twenty-four years; the war had broken its ranks and confused its principles; there were men in it now who would never have been in it had it been, that long generation through, a party of action instead of merely a party of opposition. Notable among such men were Mr. Samuel J. Randall, of Pennsylvania, and the group of members who stood with him in the House of Representatives. These men were avowed protectionists, and Mr. Randall had from 1876 to 1881 been the acknowledged congressional leader of his party. He had during those years been Speaker of the House, and by consequence master of its action in all points of legislation. Leadership in that kind passed away from him when Mr. Cleveland became President in 1885, and Mr. Carlisle, of Kentucky, became Speaker, a Democrat of the older type; but Mr. Randall's power was not gone. He still, it turned out, held the balance of power and controlled the action of the House in the matter of the tariff. Both in the Congress which preceded Mr. Cleveland's election and in that which followed it Mr. Morrison, of Illinois, had introduced proposals for the reform of the tariff which were neither radical nor disregardful of vested interests, and had pressed them

Sam'l J Randall SAMUEL JACKSON RANDALL

upon the House with arguments which lacked neither force nor the backing of opinion out of doors. An increasing surplus was being steadily piled up in the Treasury; the rates of duty which yielded the redundant revenue had been laid in time of war to meet extraordinary expenses; many of the articles which carried

the burden of the tax were necessary to people of every
rank and economic condition, notably wool and woollen
goods; relief could be obtained by reductions which
were not likely to damage any industry, or to deprive
it of any advantage which it was not abundantly able
to dispense with. But Mr. Randall led some forty
Democrats, who sat for constituencies in Pennsylvania,
Ohio, New York, California, and New Jersey, who
voted against every reduction, by whatever argument
supported, and the rest of the party, though they numbered one hundred and fifty strong, could carry nothing
against them.

It was this situation which Mr. Cleveland determined
to change, if plain speaking could change it. In December, 1887, he addressed to the new Congress chosen in
1886 a message which passed all other subjects by and
spoke only of the tariff. He asked Congress to put
theoretical questions for the nonce aside. "Our progress towards a wise conclusion," he said, "will not be
improved by dwelling upon the theories of protection
and free trade. . . . It is a condition which confronts
us,—not a theory. . . . The question of free trade
is absolutely irrelevant." "Our present tariff laws,
the vicious, inequitable, and illogical source of unnecessary taxation, ought to be at once revised and
amended," not only, he maintained, because unused
revenue was piling up, but also because consumers
were carrying an unjust burden. The message ran
strong, imperative in every sentence, and the air was
cleared upon the instant. It was the only voice of courage and decision that had been heard upon that matter
in a generation; and Mr. Randall's minority fell into
line as if confused. They had felt the compulsion of a

leader's will,—were not converted, but disciplined. The Committee of Ways and Means of the House, under the leadership of Mr. Mills, of Texas, its chairman, at once prepared a bill which attempted a systematic revision of duties, general though not radical, a measure not of free trade but of carefully planned, conservative reduction such as the President had desired; and it passed the House with only four Democratic votes cast in the negative.

The Republican Senate rejected it,—even proposed higher duties in its stead; and the existing law stood unamended. But the issue had been made up. Mr. Cleveland had given his party a distinct, unmistakable policy with which to go to the country in the presidential campaign of 1888. It accepted the issue under protest; but it accepted it. Mr. Cleveland had not taken counsel with the congressional leaders of his party before uttering his imperative message; had asked advice, indeed, of no one; had acted wholly upon his own conclusions as to what was necessary for the relief of the country. His action in the matter had filled the leading politicians of his party with dismay, its rank and file with confusion. He had been warned that to attack the protected interests of the country might cost him his re-election; but that consideration had not moved him. He believed that his party could win upon such an issue at the polls, but he would not wait to make any nice calculations on that subject; he would at least do his party the service of putting it in the right. The country relished his courage, whatever timid politicians thought of it. He stood for the moment the indisputable master of all action within the Democratic party. Its nominating convention nominated him as of course for a second

Benj Harrison

BENJAMIN HARRISON

term. The Republicans nominated General Benjamin Harrison, of Indiana, grandson to William Henry Harrison, whom death had taken untimely away to make Mr. Tyler President; and the two parties went to the country on the issue Mr. Cleveland had made.

The Democrats were defeated. The popular vote for Mr. Cleveland, indeed, exceeded that for his opponent by some one hundred and ten thousand, but Mr. Harrison had a majority of sixty-five in the electoral college (233–168). New York and Indiana had turned again to the Republicans. No northern States except Connecticut and New Jersey had voted for the Democratic candidates. Even the control of the House of Representatives was lost by the Democrats; the congressional elections gave the Republicans a working majority of about twelve. The tariff system had come to seem to that generation of voters very like a fixed part of the law of society, of the national life itself; Mr. Cleveland had not given them time enough to adjust their thought to the change he urged. There had been nowhere any sharp reaction of opinion, but everywhere in the North reaction enough to shift the balance of power once again from the Democrats to the Republicans.

On the 4th of March, 1889, Mr. Cleveland quietly gave place to Mr. Harrison and the government passed once more in all its branches into the hands of the party which had made the policy of the last twenty-eight years. But it was not the same government it had been when that party met its first serious check in 1875. It had steadied the judgment of the country in respect of parties to have a Democratic President for four years, and that President a man like Mr. Cleveland, compact of frankness, conviction, and force, no mere partisan but a man of the people, with the spirit of service strong upon him. The people had for a long time endured the deterioration of affairs under the later Republican administrations because they doubted the capacity and the principle of the Democrats. They had now learned at least that a change of parties in the administration meant no jeopardy to the government itself. The choice between parties had become once more a choice between policies merely, and affairs wore a normal aspect again,—such an aspect of peace and businesslike quiet as they had not worn since the painful shock of the Kansas-Nebraska Act. One by one the statutes which had marked the era of war and reconstruction had disappeared from the statute book: some because annulled by the Supreme Court, others by expiration, still others by repeal. Even the Tenure of Office Act had been quietly repealed after Mr. Cleveland's refusal to submit his reasons for removals to the Senate's scrutiny and review.

In 1888 the legislature of Massachusetts had adopted a method of balloting at elections borrowed directly from Australia, indirectly from England itself, which, as it spread from State to State, gave a noteworthy impetus to the purification of elections. The main features of the reform were, the facilitation of independent nominations for office outside fixed party lines, the official printing of the ballots to be used, their distribution to the voters only by sworn officers of election, and the isolation of the voter while preparing his ballot, in order perfectly to protect his privacy and independence. Opinion approved the change at once, and legislature after legislature hastened to adopt what opinion unmistakably demanded. It was one of the signs of the times. Opinion was slowly freeing itself as much as possible not only from the older party prejudices, but also from the too inquisitive management of politicians.

The foreign affairs of the government stood as they had stood when Mr. Cleveland came into office. The hostility of the Senate to his administration had rendered it impossible for him to bring any matter of negotiation to a satisfactory conclusion. The only matters of capital importance it had fallen to him to consider had concerned the fishing rights of the United States on the two coasts of the continent. Dissatisfied with the operation of those clauses of the Treaty of Washington which dealt with the Canadian fisheries, Congress had instructed the President in 1883 to give the required notice to Great Britain of the desire of the United States to abrogate them, and on the 1st of July, 1885, pursuant to Mr. Arthur's notice, they had gone out of effect. In February, 1888, under Mr. Cleveland, a new treaty regarding the fisheries had been negotiated; but the Senate had rejected it. The question which arose on the other side of the continent concerned the rights of the United States over the seal fisheries of the north Pacific. The United States claimed that the purchase of Alaska from Russia in 1867 had brought with it the right to protect the seals of Bering Sea against capture or destruction, having brought with it exclusive jurisdiction over that sea. England denied the right and the jurisdiction; but the government passed out of Mr. Cleveland's hands before the matter could be brought to a definitive formulation and issue. It passed to Mr. Harrison along with all other pending questions of policy and administration.

Authorities now begin to grow scarce. Mr. Edward Stanwood's *History of the Presidency* still affords an excellent sketch of political conditions; Edward McPherson's *Handbook of Politics* still records the chief political happenings; Mr. Francis Newton Thorpe brings his *Constitutional History of the United States* down through this period; Appleton's invaluable *Annual Cyclopaedia* makes careful record of events; and the more serious magazines of the country, such as *The Atlantic Monthly, The North American Review, The Forum, The Nation, The New Princeton Review, The Political Science Quarterly*, and the *Quarterly Journal of Economics* furnish reviews and discussions of almost all the principal public transactions of the time. *The New Princeton Review* contains an exhaustive Record of Events (1885–1888), which, after 1888, is continued in *The Political Science Quarterly*, in which *The New Princeton Review* was merged. Mr. S. S. Cox's *Three Decades of Federal Legislation* covers the years down to 1885; Mr. Hugh McCulloch's *Men and Measures of Half a Century* runs a little way into the period of this chapter; Mr. John Sherman's *Recollections of Forty Years in House, Senate, and Cabinet* covers all of it; and the collected *Works* of Mr. George William Curtis shed excellent light on many of the more serious questions of the times. Mr. John Clark Ridpath has prepared *The Life and Works of James A. Garfield* in such a way as to afford some guidance in the history of the time.

Mr. A. S. Bolles's *Financial History of the United States* (to 1885), Mr. Carroll D. Wright's *Industrial Evolution of the United States*, Professor F. W. Taussig's *Tariff History of the United States* (to 1883) and *Silver Situation in the United States*, and Mr. David A. Wells's *Recent Economic Changes* are our chief authorities on matters fiscal, financial, and economic. Mr. C. Juglar has written *A Brief History of Panics;* Mr. H. Lambert a sketch of *The Progress of Civil Service Reform in the United States;* Mr. C. B. Elliott a recital of the principal facts with regard to *The United States and the Northeastern Fisheries;* and Mr. Eugene Schuyler a treatise on *American Diplomacy*, which is an excellent manual of the larger international concerns of the country. Mr. Henry Jones Ford's *Rise and Growth of American Politics*, Mr. Lauros G. McConachie's *Congressional Committees*, and Miss M. P. Follett's *Speaker of the House of Representatives* still serve us in explaining congressional influence and procedure and party action.

The *sources* here, as in the last chapter, are *The Congressional Record*, the various series of *Documents* published by House and Senate, the *Messages and Papers of the Presidents*, the *Statutes at Large*, and the newspapers and other periodicals of the time.

CHAPTER III

THE END OF A CENTURY

MR. HARRISON entered office amidst signs of a new age. The Republican party which had put him forward was not the Republican party of the war and of reconstruction but the Republican party of the new day of industrial revolution. Old questions had fallen out of sight or were transformed by changes in the nation itself; new questions pressed for solution which had in them no flavor of the older passion of party politics. Mr. Cleveland's four years of office had altered many things. For the mass of voters they had altered the very principle of choice between parties. That choice turned now once again upon questions of the day, not upon the issues of a war long ago fought out or of a reconstruction of southern society which politicians had touched only to mar and embarrass. A full century had gone by since the government of the nation was set up. Within that century, it now began to appear, fundamental questions of governmental structure and political authority had been settled and the country drawn together to a common life. Henceforth matters were to be in debate which concerned the interests of society everywhere, in one section as in another, questions which were without geographical boundary, questions of the modern world, touching nations no less than communities which fancied themselves to lie apart.

And yet a new sectionalism began to show itself, not political, but economic. In 1890, for the first time, the census takers found it impossible to trace upon their maps any line which marked the front of settlement between the Mississippi and the rising heights of the Rockies. Hitherto there had always been a "frontier" within the body of the continent, a line along which ran the outposts of settlement, and beyond that, between the newest settlements and the slopes of the Pacific, a well defined space as yet unpeopled. But now such regions had lost their definite outlines. Here and there were yet vacant spaces, some of them, it might be, as extensive in area as a great State: some tract of desert, some region which promised neither the fruits of the earth nor hidden wealth of minerals; but for the rest population had diffused itself so generally that frontiers had disappeared and the differences between region and region seemed little more than differences in the density of population. And yet there were lines of separation, none the less, which no census taker could draw but to which statesmen of necessity gave heed, which were as significant as anything the older maps had shown. The careful student of economic conditions might almost have made a sketch upon the map of the new divisions of the country,—divisions of interest: those most fundamental of all differences, differences in the stage of development. Any observant traveller might remark them as he moved from the teeming eastern seaports into the West or South. From the Atlantic seaboard to the Mississippi and the great lakes there stretched, north of Mason and Dixon's line, a region substantially homogeneous in all the larger interests of trade and industry, not unlike European countries in the development of its resources and the complex diversification of its life; but beyond it, to the west and south, lay regions and communities of another kind, at another stage of development, agricultural, for the most part, up to the very ridges of the Rockies, or else set apart to some special interest like that of mining or of cattle raising on the great scale. Throughout all the vast continent, to the east of the Mississippi as to the west, contrasts were, indeed, modulated; hardly anywhere was the transition sharp from one set of social and economic conditions to another. But, taken upon the large view, they were very great, very radical, very significant, openly prophetic of differences of opinion and of interest.

Settlement had crossed the continent, but always with a thin and scattered front, its masses neither homogeneous nor uniform, its processes hasty, imperfect, crude until the third or fourth generation. In many places settlers were yet but in the first generation. Line after line to be found upon the decennial maps of the census office, to mark the frontier of fixed settlement decade by decade, was still to be traced in differences of habit and development between community and community from east to west, not yet effaced by the feet of those who had crossed them to make homes beyond. Communities were still making and to be made. Conditions as if of a first day of settlement, conditions such as had once existed upon the coast of the Atlantic in the far-away days of the first colonies, conditions which had been shifted generation by generation from east to west across the whole breadth of the great con-

tinent, were still to be observed in hastily built towns at the far West, upon broad cattle ranches, in rough mining villages, in new regions upon the vast western plains where the plough had but just begun to break the surface of the virgin land into fruitful furrows. The land itself, by reason of its own infinite variety of character and resource, commanded changes of life and diversity of occupation. There were broad tracts of country which were entirely without cities or centres of population or any industry which brought men together in intimate co-operative groups, tracts given over by nature to the farmer and the grazier. There were States where communities sharply contrasted in life and motive were set side by side, to the sore perplexity of those who sought to make their laws and reconcile their interests: placer mines which poured the refuse of their operations down the slopes of the western mountains upon smiling farms which they were like to ruin; towns perched high within the peaks of the towering Rockies, where precious metals were to be found, which yet lay within the same political boundaries with keepers of sheep and cattle in the plains below; centres of trade and of manufacture, lying upon some great watercourse or by the coasts of the western ocean, which seemed hardly more than huge trading posts on the routes of commerce from east to west, from west to east, so little intimate part did they have in the life of the rural people amidst whose prairie farms or broad orchards of fruit they were set.

It was these differences, this lack of homogeneity, this diversity of habit, interest, and point of view which had begun to tell upon the politics of the country with the ending of the war and of the processes of reconstruction, and which now began to be decisive in the formulation of party programmes. The South, with the passing away of slavery and of the leadership of the greater landholders, bred in an elder school of politics, had become like the newer regions of the West in motive and opinion. It, too, was predominantly agricultural. Its farmers were not the aristocratic planters of the elder society which the war had destroyed, but were for the most part men of the class from which Andrew Johnson had come: plain men who did not stand for the old traditions, who had not themselves owned slaves and who had felt none of the *esprit* of privilege that had ruled affairs in the days gone by; men as new in politics, as new in political thinking and constructive purpose, as much bound within the narrow limits of their own experience as the men of the western farms. Any one who noted how the tenets of the Farmers' Alliance and the new and radical heresies with regard to money took root there could see how the South had in fact become itself a new region in all that touched its social organization and its political thinking, a region as it were of recent settlement and late development so far as all the new order of the nation's life was concerned. Errors of opinion began to prevail there, as in the new regions of the West, like those which had swept through the crude colonies in the unquiet days which preceded and followed the War for Independence: hopes that the credit of the government itself might in some manner be placed at the disposal of the farmers in the handling and marketing of their crops, demands for a "cheap" currency, of paper or of silver, which should be easier to get and easier to pay debts with than the gold which lay so secure in the vaults

of the banks and of the federal Treasury. The communities from which such demands came lay remote
from the centres of trade where men could see in the
transactions of every day what the real laws of credit,
of value, and of exchange must always be, whether
legislators would have them so or not. Moreover,
they felt profoundly, though vaguely, the economic uneasiness of the time, the novel power of the railways
to determine markets and prices and margins of profit,
the rising influence of great aggregations of capital
in the controlling industries of the country, the providential oversight of banks and of those who made
the arrangements of credit and exchange. Every
farmer, every rural shopkeeper and trader, every man
who attempted manufacture upon a small scale felt at
a cruel disadvantage, and, letting his thoughts run only
upon his own experience and observation, dreamed of
bettering his chances by an abundant issue of at least
the cheaper of the two monetary metals by the government itself, in order that bankers and capitalists might
no longer keep poor men in bondage.

It was the rise and spread of such opinions that the
Republicans, now once again in power, in Congress
as in the presidency, had to face. There was as good
reason for the apostles of the new radicalism to hope
to establish themselves in the counsels of the Republican
party as to hope to control the action of the Democrats.
Republican constituencies were touched with the new
heresies, in many parts of the country, as sharply as
Democratic constituencies, and the one party was not
more expressly committed than the other against the
policies proposed. The Whigs, from whom chiefly
the Republicans took their political lineage, had stood

always for a sound and stable currency; but so also had the Democrats, with their unbroken party history since the days of Mr. Jefferson himself. The difference between them had been hardly more than this, that the Whigs wished to use the instrumentality of a national bank in the management of the public finances, while the Democrats, rejecting a bank, had sought to make the Treasury in all things independent of private business interests. The Democrats had sought to break all connection between the federal government and the banks, but they had never thought to touch the credit of the country with the hopeless demoralization of a depreciated and fluctuating currency by any imprudent law of coinage or by any substitution of a body of paper issues for the accepted monetary metals. General Jackson had come perilously near to wrecking the whole fabric of credit in order to put all payments to the government upon a gold basis. No doubt it was the questionable decisions of the Supreme Court of the United States in the legal tender cases which had opened the minds of politicians to rash experiment in the field of financial legislation. Those decisions justified the government in making its own mere promises legal tender in the payment of both public and private debts. The immense issues of the war time were made in their reasoning to seem compatible with the ordinary processes of public finance. Legislators got a novel and misleading sense of power in the creation of values. The country was ready to believe that such measures as the Bland Silver Bill of 1878, passed through Congress by votes drawn from both parties, might come from either party, should the movement of opinion in that direction but grow strong enough. The Democrats, it might be, stood nearer to the mass of the people in such matters, and undoubtedly drew their chief strength from the West and South, where the new opinions showed themselves strongest and most aggressive; but the Republicans, though they drew their support chiefly from the industrial and commercial centres of the country, showed also an uneasy fear lest they should seem to fail to meet popular doctrine half way. They were not loath, observers began to remark, to play to the populace upon occasion.

That impression was not a little strengthened by the action of the new Republican Congress. In midsummer, 1890, an Act was passed which put the coinage of silver and its use as a medium of exchange on a new footing, but which by no means reversed the policy of the government or turned away from experiment. It in set terms repealed the Bland Act of 1878, and it put a limit of one year upon the continued coinage of the silver bullion purchased by the Treasury; but it did not discontinue the purchase of silver by the government. It provided that the Treasury should each month purchase four and a half million ounces of silver at its market price; that the bullion thus bought should be paid for in Treasury notes of the United States; that after July 1, 1891, the silver purchased should no longer be coined, except so far as might be necessary in order to supply the Treasury with coin enough to redeem its notes; that the notes issued in payment for the bullion should be legal tender in the satisfaction of all debts; and that they should be redeemable in either gold or silver at the discretion of the Secretary of the Treasury. The Act declared it to be "the established policy of the United States to maintain the two metals at a parity with each other" at a fixed ratio determined by law. It was with a view to maintaining their parity that the Secretary of the Treasury was bidden use his discretion

JOHN SHERMAN

in the redemption of the notes, being expected to see to it that the one metal was not suffered wholly to supplant the other, or that the one should not be made more difficult to obtain than the other. Mr. John Sherman, the honored senator from Ohio, a man whom business men the country over looked upon as a careful student of affairs, and particularly of public finance, had fathered the measure. It was a significant political sign of the times that he should thus take part in an effort to give silver an artificial value, despite the movement, the irresistible movement, of the market. The ratio of value between gold and silver fixed by statute was not the ratio fixed by the law of supply and demand. The price of silver rose a little at first, under the influence of the Act, but it could not be kept up. The law of supply and demand was not checked in its operation. It governed the value of the metal as of all other things bought and sold. The statutes of no single government could set the efficacy of that law aside. The experience of the one-time monetary union of the Latin countries of Europe seemed to make it unlikely that even international agreement in matters of coinage could keep the values of the two metals to a fixed and stable ratio. Mr. Sherman and his colleagues both in House and Senate must have been conscious that they were playing to the galleries.

All policy came, as in General Grant's day, as in Johnson's day, from the leaders of Congress. Mr. Harrison did not possess the gifts of leadership. A man of unquestionable character and gifted above most of his predecessors with the power to think and speak clearly, impressively, and to the point upon every public issue, a man of culture, thoughtfully read in affairs and trained by long experience in the public service, he utterly lacked personal charm and the power either to persuade or to please the men about him. His manner was cold and distant; he seemed neither to give nor to invite confidence. A cool air of orderly routine seemed always to pervade the executive chambers of the White House. It was not a place of intimate counsel where leaders conferred, but a place, rather, where the public duties of the President were performed in a sort of dignified seclusion. There was a pleasing independence in the way in which Mr. Harrison showed his good conscience and careful diligence in affairs, but no warm impulse came from him which the leaders in Congress felt constrained to reckon with. The legislative acts of the majority showed, consequently, no single informing purpose. Rank and file were apparently looking for safe ground rather than framing systematic and consistent policies.

The question of the tariff held the chief place of attention in debate. Before the close of May, 1890, the House, under the leadership of Mr. William McKinley, the chairman of its Committee of Ways and Means, had passed a new tariff Act, considerably increasing the protective duties, especially upon wool and woollen goods. The tariff had been the chief issue upon which the elections of 1888 had turned, at which the Republicans had won their majority. Mr. Cleveland had made the issue by his unexpected, outspoken message of December, 1887. The Republican leaders deemed their victory at the polls a sort of mandate not merely to maintain but also to strengthen the system of protective duties; and the Ways and Means Committee of the House had made it its first task to prepare a bill which should satisfy the expectations of the country. The House accepted the bill after but two weeks of debate. The Senate kept it all summer under consideration and so altered it before finally adopting it in September that a conference between the two houses became necessary before an agreement could be reached; but by October 1 it had become law. It had passed by a strict party vote in each House. Even members of the Republican majority had had uneasy misgivings as they watched the movements of opinion out-of-doors. It was not certain that they had not won in the elections as much because Mr. Cleveland had disappointed some of his independent supporters by proving himself more of a party man than they cared to be as because he had demanded a revision of the tariff. There was at least candor and a definite party purpose in what the new majority had done, however. Their party was once more unequivocally committed upon one of the chief questions of the day.

It was growing from year to year more and more difficult to calculate, more and more difficult to guide the movements of opinion. The new age of growth which had followed the war showed a quickened pace of change. The years 1889–1890 saw six new States added to the roster of the Union: North Dakota, South Dakota, Montana, Washington, Idaho, and Wyoming, and thoughtful men perceived how significant a thing it was that but five Territories remained in all the broad continent, with scattered Reservations here and there in the farther West, set apart for the redmen. In 1889 the government had purchased of the tribes even a part of the Indian Territory which lay within the circle of Kansas, Arkansas, and Texas, to be thrown open to white settlers,—the fairest portion of it, Oklahoma, the Beautiful Land which lay almost at its heart; and all the country had heard how mad a rush there had been across its borders to secure its coveted acres. A host

THE RUSH OF SETTLERS INTO OKLAHOMA

of settlers fifty thousand strong had encamped upon its very boundary lines to await the signal to go in and take possession.   At noon on the 22d of April, 1889, at the sound of a bugle blown to mark the hour set by the President's proclamation, the waiting multitude surged madly in, and the Territory was peopled in a single day. It was the old, familiar process of first occupation and settlement carried out as if in a play, the story of the nation's making in a brief epitome.   Its suddenness, its eagerness, its resistless movement of excited men marked in dramatic fashion the end of the day of settlement.   The best parts of the continent, save isolated Reservations here and there, were taken up; and the stream of population was dammed at their borders only by the barriers of law.   When they were removed it would spring forward like a flood.

The census of 1890 showed the population of the country increased to 62,622,250, an addition of 12,466,467 within the decade.   Immigrants poured steadily in as before, but with an alteration of stock which students of affairs marked with uneasiness.   Throughout the century men of the sturdy stocks of the north of Europe had made up the main strain of foreign blood which was every year added to the vital working force of the country, or else men of the Latin-Gallic stocks of France and northern Italy; but now there came multitudes of men of the lowest class from the south of Italy and men of the meaner sort out of Hungary and Poland, men out of the ranks where there was neither skill nor energy nor any initiative of quick intelligence; and they came in numbers which increased from year to year, as if the countries of the south of Europe were disburdening themselves of the more sordid and hapless elements

212

of their population, the men whose standards of life and of work were such as American workmen had never dreamed of hitherto. The people of the Pacific coast had clamored these many years against the admission of immigrants out of China, and in May, 1892, got at last what they wanted, a federal statute which practically excluded from the United States all Chinese who had not already acquired the right of residence;

OKLAHOMA ON THE DAY OF OPENING

and yet the Chinese were more to be desired, as workmen if not as citizens, than most of the coarse crew that came crowding in every year at the eastern ports. They had, no doubt, many an unsavory habit, bred unwholesome squalor in the crowded quarters where they most abounded in the western seaports, and seemed separated by their very nature from the people among whom they had come to live; but it was their skill, their intelligence, their hardy power of labor, their knack at succeeding and driving duller rivals out, rather than their alien habits, that made them feared and hated

213

and led to their exclusion at the prayer of the men they were likely to displace should they multiply. The unlikely fellows who came in at the eastern ports were tolerated because they usurped no place but the very lowest in the scale of labor.

The year of the McKinley tariff and of the Sherman Act for the purchase of silver had brought fresh congressional elections, and after that there had been no more important party legislation. The Chinese exclusion Act had been no party measure, but a concession which both parties were willing to make to the opinion of the Pacific coast. The elections of 1890 had created in the House, instead of the slender Republican majority of a dozen votes, a Democratic majority of close upon one hundred and fifty. The tide was beginning to run which in 1892 swept the Republicans altogether from power. Once again, for the third time, when it came to the nomination of presidential candidates, the Democrats nominated Mr. Cleveland; for a second time the Republicans nominated Mr. Harrison; and the result of the elections of 1888 was reversed. The popular vote for Mr. Cleveland exceeded that for Mr. Harrison by less than three hundred thousand in a total vote of more than twelve million, but the turning about of opinion had been singularly widespread. Every State accounted doubtful in its choice between parties had given its electoral vote to Mr. Cleveland, and his minority of sixty-five in the electoral college of 1888 was turned into a majority of one hundred and ten. Colorado, Nevada, Oregon, Idaho, North Dakota, and Kansas had cast their votes for the candidates of the People's party. In most of those States the Democrats had nominated no presidential electors; they had satisfied

OKLAHOMA FOUR WEEKS AFTER THE OPENING

themselves with supporting the growing People's party, pleased if by any means they might discomfit the Republicans and half inclined to accept the opinions of their new allies in preference to the opinions of their own leaders.

The People's party, which the newspapers of the country promptly dubbed "Populist," had put forth a platform which demanded that the federal government should itself acquire the ownership of all railways, telegraphs, and telephones, that the free coinage of gold and silver at the ratio of sixteen to one should be accorded by law, that a graduated income tax should be established, postal savings banks created, and all lands held by aliens, or by corporations in excess of their needs, reclaimed,—a radical programme which jumped with the humor of hundreds of thousands of workingmen and farmers the country over. It was noted how universal a defection there was from the Republican ranks in the West. Those who knew how opinion moved there said that even those who had voted for the Republican electors and the Republican nominees for Congress had done so rather out of habit or conservative temper or the hope that time and the influences of opinion would bring their leaders to a creed and policy like that of the advocates of free coinage and of governmental restrictions upon the railways and upon organized capital than because they still believed in the doctrines professed from of old by their party.

There was apparently no reason why they should not entertain the hope, at least with regard to the coinage. The platforms of both the Republican and the Democratic nominating conventions spoke very strongly for the continued use of both gold and silver as money and for some arrangement which should maintain them at an equality in value, and the language which they held in the matter might without too much ingenuity be made to square with almost any policy. The Re-

SAN FRANCISCO FROM THE BAY

publican platform spoke of the use of both the metals "with such restrictions and under such provisions, to be determined by legislation, as will secure the maintenance of the parity of values of the two metals, so that the purchasing and debt-paying power of the dollar, whether of silver, gold, or paper, shall be at all times

217

equal." The Democratic platform spoke of making
the units of the coinage of the two metals "of equal
intrinsic and exchangeable value, adjusted through
international agreement or by such safeguards of legislation as shall ensure the maintenance of the parity of
the two metals and the equal power of every dollar at
all times in the markets and in the payment of debts."
No doubt experiment was in the air and radical experi-
menters might, if they were but shrewd and persistent
enough, gain control of either party as opinion made
head. After the party conventions had met and spoken
(July 1, 1892) the Republican Senate passed a bill which
provided for the free coinage of all silver brought to
the mints, the repeal of the Sherman Act, and the coinage of all the bullion purchased under its terms. The
Democratic House declined to consider the bill, by a
vote of 154 to 136, but rather, it was suspected, because its leaders thought it prudent to await the result
of the presidential election than because there lacked
advocates of free coinage enough to pass it.

For the moment Democratic advocates of "free silver" stood embarrassed by their candidate. Before the
nominating conventions had met Mr. Cleveland had
spoken his mind very clearly, very positively, as was
his wont, upon the monetary question. He had given
out for publication a brief letter which spoke in terms
which no one could possibly mistake against any such
tampering with the standards of value as the People's
party and their secret partisans within the Democratic
and Republican ranks desired. His personal friends
had wished him to make no public announcement of
his views, had begged him not unnecessarily to commit
himself upon a question upon which his nomination

INSIDE A TREASURY VAULT AT WASHINGTON.   TAKING BAGS OF
SILVER OUT TO BE WEIGHED

might turn; but he had rejected their counsel with a sort of scorn and had uttered his conviction in the matter with that fearless decision and that unequivocal way of speech which the country most admired in him. He had been nominated, nevertheless, taken upon his own terms, and the country's knowledge of his conviction in that critical matter had probably saved his party the discrediting suspicion which the fusion of Democrats with Populists upon the Pacific coast might have brought upon it.

The country had never needed a man of his fibre more. It had reached a sharp crisis of opinion, and crises in affairs followed fast which no man without courage and steadfast character could have swung the government clear of. The four years which followed Mr. Cleveland's second election were among the most remarkable years of peace the country had ever seen. Disorders of the most serious character, alike in business and in politics, had within that brief space their sharp culmination; foreign questions of the most delicate and critical kind unexpectedly arose; society itself seemed upheaved by forces which threatened it with lasting injury; and amidst parties which seemed without leadership or cohesion the President alone stood firm and spoke definite counsel.

The Democrats had come into power again upon a definite issue, the issue to which Mr. Cleveland had given such sharp definition in his famous message of 1887, the issue of the tariff. Upon no other matter so much as upon that had the voting turned; upon no other matter did the Democrats bear so unmistakable a commission from the country. But Mr. Cleveland saw that the matter which called first and most

imperatively for action was the financial situation of the government and of the country. The financial experiments of the last fourteen years had begun to bear fruit in abundance. There were outstanding some five hundred million currency notes of the government which it was obliged upon demand to redeem in gold; and yet even when once redeemed they were not cancelled. The law directed that they should be issued again, to come back once more, if their holders chose to present them, to be redeemed in gold. Gold was constantly demanded, and in immense sums which seemed to grow ominously from quarter to quarter, not only for profitable export and to pay foreign balances, but also as a safe fund against what might happen when the crash should come which every observant man feared to be at hand. The government was obliged by the Sherman Act of 1890 to buy four and a half million ounces of silver every month and pay for them in notes which the Secretary of the Treasury knew that he must redeem in gold on demand if he would keep panic off. So soon as the government ceased paying in gold the artificial "parity" between gold and silver which the laws sought to maintain would be destroyed; silver would, in effect, become the only standard of values, the only medium of exchange; every piece of property in the country, tangible or intangible, would lose half its value; and credit would collapse. And yet how could the government keep itself supplied with gold? Very few of its debtors were obliged to pay in that coin; it could replenish its diminishing stock only by borrowing, and could borrow only by the issue of bonds made payable "in coin" of which lenders might well grow shy as they saw politicians grow less and less

A SILVER MINING TOWN, GEORGETOWN, COLORADO

firm in their resistance to the demands of the advocates of the free coinage of silver.

It was clear enough what Mr. Cleveland thought and intended, but it was by no means clear that Congress would willingly lend him its aid. He led a party in which silver advocates abounded, men who lived remote from the seats of trade and knew nothing of its laws. It was not certain that the Republicans were any stiffer in their resistance to the pressure of radical opinion in the matter of the coinage. What might happen when it came to actual legislation by Congress who could foresee? Early in June, 1893, Mr. Cleveland announced his purpose to call Congress together in extraordinary session for the consideration of the finances. On the 26th of June the authorities of India closed their mints to the free coinage of silver, and the price of the metal dropped as it had never dropped before. On the 30th of June the President summoned Congress to meet on the 7th of August. The silver mines of the West were promptly closed, and thousands of miners were thrown out of employment, to be taken care of and become a serious menace to order in the nearby cities, into which they crowded hungry and forlorn. The greatest excitement prevailed in the West. Before Congress assembled conventions of the advocates of silver had been held in Denver and Chicago which protested vehemently against Mr. Cleveland's evident intention to have the law which obliged the Treasury to purchase silver set aside, and declared that he was acting in concert with the eastern bankers to thrust silver altogether out of use as money. They demanded that, should the Sherman Act be repealed, the free coinage of silver should be substituted. When Congress assembled it was noted that the ordinary party lines seemed for a little while almost to disappear. The advocates of silver coinage acted together in both houses without regard to their differences upon other subjects, and acted with the ardor of men who serve a cause.

Mr. Crisp, whom the House chose Speaker, was of the

BULLION AT THE AMERICAN SMELTER, LEADVILLE, COLORADO

silver group within his party, but felt bound, as the party's official leader in matters of legislation, to give the President all the support the authority of the speakership could afford. Mr. Cleveland asked for a single, specific act of relief, the repeal of the purchasing clause of the Sherman Act of 1890, and Mr. Crisp held together as he could the members who were inclined to meet the crisis as the needs of the Treasury seemed to demand. Public opinion out of doors pressed uncomfortably, too. Panic had already come in the money market, and the business of the country was suffering the consequences. A repealing bill was introduced on August 11th, and on the 28th was passed, by a vote of 240 to 110, so sensitively did the House feel the airs of opinion and the necessity for acting in good faith with the President for the relief of the Treasury. But the Senate would make no such show of compliance. There the silver men mustered so strong that it was not clear until the autumn had come that a majority for repeal could be obtained at all, and every delay known to the leisurely rules of the body was made use of to hold action off. Meanwhile the country took the consequences. Credit collapsed; loans could nowhere be obtained; the very currency seemed to disappear, being hoarded and kept out of the currents of trade in such extraordinary quantities that those who needs must have it were obliged to pay a premium for its use and the banks used clearing house certificates in its stead. Failure followed failure. The very processes of manufacture stood still. Business men knew not what to do. The business of the country was sound; its resources were untouched. There had been no speculative flurries, no irregular operations that could justify panic or impair confidence. Nothing was awry except the public finances: men could not be sure of the value of the money they handled. It was not certain that the government would not put all exchanges upon the silver basis. The worst was over before the Senate acted. Business of sheer necessity recovered its tone; and when at last, at the very end of October, the repeal became law, trade and manufacture began to stir again with reassuring evidences of returning life.

But the results of panic and failure were not stayed. A Treasury report of the 19th of October showed a falling off in the revenues, as compared with the estimates, during the preceding three months, which would mean, if continued, a deficit of $50,000,000 for the fiscal year. Every industry was slackened, imports had fallen off, foreign capitalists were withdrawing their investments. It was hardly a propitious time at which to undertake a revision of the tariff. The Democrats were pledged, nevertheless, to undertake it. That was the only reform to which they were explicitly pledged; they had majorities in both houses, and Mr. Cleveland was President. The financial legislation most immediately and imperatively needed was out of the way, and the field was apparently clear before them. They could not face the country again upon the tariff issue should they fail to redeem their promises in the matter of the reduction of the duties. The House Committee on Ways and Means had begun the preparation of a tariff bill during the special session at which the battle against the purchase of silver had been fought out, and before the time set for the regular session of December had made public the terms of the measure they meant to propose. In the House there was little difficulty in pressing it to its passage. Reported early in January, it had passed by the 1st of February, together with an internal revenue bill meant to make good the estimated reductions in the receipts at the ports. It was a genuine measure of reform. It proceeded upon the principle that the raw materials of manufacture ought for the most part to be entirely freed from duty; that there should be throughout the whole list of dutiable articles as considerable a reduction of duties as a prudent regard for vested interests would permit; and that duties should be *ad valorem* rather than specific in order that the burden of the consumer might in every case be clearly calculable. Coal, iron ore, and sugar were put upon the free list. The internal revenue bill associated with the revision embodied, as its chief features, a tax upon incomes and an increased excise on distilled spirits.

The trouble came, as before, in the Senate. There the disintegration of the Democratic party was evident as it was not evident in the House. Senators allowed themselves to be attached to particular interests, put party pledges aside very lightly, acted like men who had forgot the compulsions of political principle and played each for his own benefit. Before the measure got out of their hands they had altered it almost beyond recognition. They had put in once more an elaborate schedule of duties on sugar, had taken coal and iron ore from the free list, had changed *ad valorem* duties to specific, and had all through the bill made alterations which increased the rates of duty proposed by the House, each senator exerting himself, as it seemed, to secure protection or advantage for the industries of his own State. The average rate of duty under the McKinley Act had been about 50 *per cent.*; the House bill had reduced it to about 35½; the changes made in the Senate increased it to about 37. It was not the general increase of rates effected in the Senate that held the attention of the country so much as the very noticeable activity of a group of senators in the interest of the sugar manufacturers and dealers. There was manifestly no thought of either party interest or public duty

DON M. DICKINSON

in what they did; they were acting in some private interest, it was to be feared upon some private motive,— were heeding, not their party leaders, but the representatives of a particular industry who had obtained a hold upon them which could not be shaken. Their headstrong, stubborn rejection of political obligations wrecked the Democratic programme and utterly discredited their party. The House, in despair of getting anything better, accepted the mutilated bill which came from their hands (August 13, 1894), and the President suffered it to become law without his signature.

The internal revenue Act, with its provision for an income tax, had gone through both houses as a part of the tariff measure; but it stood as law only nine months. The income tax was at once challenged in the federal courts, test cases were hurried to a conclusion, and on the 20th of May, 1895, the Supreme Court declared it unconstitutional. It was a reversal of former decisions. A tax upon incomes had been among the innumerable taxes adopted to support the war for the Union, and the court had then deemed the tax permissible. But it now took another position. The tax was, it said, a direct tax; the constitution provided that direct taxes should be apportioned among the several States in proportion to their population; and, inasmuch as this tax was not so apportioned, it was unconstitutional. Without the income tax the deficit caused by the reductions of duty just effected could not be made good, and the financial position of the government became more difficult than ever. There was not likely to be revenue enough to meet the expenditures, which Congress had voted as lavishly as if the Treasury were full to overflowing.

The repeal of the silver purchasing clause of the Sherman Act had only in small part relieved the embarrassments of the Treasury. There was still the unending difficulty of maintaining the gold reserve,

THOMAS FRANCIS BAYARD

the "endless chain" of Treasury notes coming in to be redeemed in gold and immediately paid out again to be presented at their holders' pleasure for more gold, always being paid for and yet never redeemed. The President, in a special message of the 28th of January,

231

1895, very earnestly requested Congress to authorize the Secretary of the Treasury to sell bonds for the replenishment of the gold reserve which should be explicitly payable in gold at their maturity and therefore sure of sale at a handsome premium, and also to authorize the retirement of the notes, instead of their reissue, upon redemption, in order to stop in part at least the inroads upon the reserve. But the houses would do nothing. The advocates of silver coinage were strong enough in both houses to block what legislation they chose, and regarded Mr. Cleveland as their arch opponent. They would allow nothing to be done to relieve the embarrassments of the administration.

For the first time since the war for the Union, for the first time in thirty-two years, the Democrats controlled both houses and the presidency; and yet Mr. Cleveland seemed like a President without a party. Some attributed it to his lack of tact, his aggressive independence in action, his too confident initiative, his way of using his power as if he were under no obligation to his party associates to consult or consider them. He did, in fact, hold upon occasion very strictly to the literary theory of the constitution, the theory which the makers of the constitution had accepted from M. Montesquieu. He regarded the legislative and executive departments of the government as by intention set apart from each other and meant each to exercise an independent judgment and discretion in the performance of the duties which fell to it, co-operating, indeed, but not compounding, not parts of a party system, ministry and majority, but the balanced checks of a carefully devised mechanism of legal action. He had never had the point of view with regard to executive functions which is natural to a member of a legislative body. As mayor, as governor, and as President, he had always conceived it his function to check legislative action rather than guide it, had thought of himself always as an administrative officer, not as a party leader. It was noticeable that he made

WILLIAM FREEMAN VILAS

up his cabinets upon that theory. In his first cabinet there had been men like Mr. Thomas F. Bayard, of Delaware, Mr. Lucius Q. C. Lamar, of Mississippi, Mr. William F. Vilas, of Wisconsin, and Mr. Don M. Dickinson, of Michigan, who had been chosen in accordance with well recognized precedents in such matters: because of their service in party counsels; but the rest were men, so far as might be, of his own personal selection, whom he chose, not for their influence

233

among politicians or in political canvass, but because he knew their efficiency as men of business. In his second cabinet the element of personal choice was still more noticeable. The Secretary of State had been a distinguished federal judge, and had been in the cabinet of Mr. Arthur,—had but the other day turned from his former Republican associates to support Mr. Cleveland, a fresh recruit in the Democratic ranks. The Secretary of War had in his previous administration been Mr. Cleveland's private secretary. The Postmaster General had been his partner in Buffalo in the practice of law. The Attorney General was one of the leaders of the bar of Massachusetts, no politician, a great lawyer merely. The President's object was to surround himself, not with a party council, but with capable heads of departments.

No doubt he seemed to members of his party in Congress a trifle too separate and absolute. He did not seem to regard it as any part of his constitutional business to be forever arranging agreements between the Executive and the houses. He held to a very strict principle of duty in every matter upon which he was approached, deeming his connection with his party in some sense broken or suspended so long as he was President, in order that he might serve the country as a whole without any too sensitive scruples as to the effect of his decisions upon coming elections. It was inevitable, since he held himself so and swung free of party advice when he pleased, that he should seem to put his own judgment above that of the congressmen who approached him. Sometimes he would patiently confer, persuade, and come to terms of agreement; but at other times he would decline with a noticeable touch of impatience to take any part in the arrangement of legislative plans, and in effect bid members of the houses go their own way while he went his.

But his action in such matters grew out of the situation in which he found himself as much as out of his theory with regard to his office and his natural tem-

L. Q. C. Lamar   L. Q. C. LAMAR

perament in dealing with men who did not act upon fixed conviction, as he did, but rather upon considerations of political or personal expediency. His party was in fact going to pieces and turning away from him, under the compulsion of forces over which he had no control. The business of the country had fallen dull and inactive because of the financial disquietude of the time. A great poverty and depression had come

235

upon the western mining regions and upon the agricultural regions of the West and South. Prices had fallen;
crops had failed. Drought swept the western plains
clean of their golden harvests. Farmers in the districts most stricken could not so much as buy clothes
for their backs, and went clad in the sacks into which
they would have put their grain had they had any,
their feet wrapped about with pieces of coarse sack-
cloth for lack of shoes. Men of the poorer sort were
idle everywhere, and filled with a sort of despair. All
the large cities and manufacturing towns teemed with
unemployed workingmen who were with the utmost
difficulty kept from starvation by the systematic efforts
of organized charity. In many cities public works
were undertaken upon an extensive scale to give them
employment. In the spring of 1894 "armies of the
unemployed" began to gather in the western country
for the purpose of marching upon Washington, like
mendicant hosts, to make known to the government
itself, face to face, the wants of the people. The dramatic plan seems to have been originated by one Coxey,
of Massillon, Ohio, who announced that he would lead
an "Army of the Commonweal of Christ" to Washington to propose that the government issue $500,000,000
in greenbacks to be paid out for work upon the public
roads, in order that the country might at one and the
same time be supplied with serviceable highways and
abundant money. On the 25th of March he actually
set out, and by the 1st of May was at the capital. A
hundred men began the journey with him, and their
ranks had swelled to three hundred and fifty by the
time they entered Washington. They made no disturbance. Most of the towns and villages on their

COXEY AND HIS ARMY APPROACHING WASHINGTON

way supplied them with food, partly out of charitable
good humor, partly in order to speed them on their way
and be quit of them, lest they should linger or grow ugly
in temper; good natured sympathizers and men who
wished to see the comedy played out subscribed funds
for their most urgent needs. The painful farce was
soon over. Their errand of course came to nothing.
They reached Washington to find that there was nothing that they could do, and dispersed. But their example was imitated with less harmless results. Other
"armies" gathered, in more sullen mood, to take their
turn at marching and living upon the country as they
went. Some started from the faraway coasts of the
Pacific. Railway trains were seized to afford them
transportation across the mountains and across the long
plains where marching would be most painful, tedious,

237

and unprofitable. Country-sides experienced a sort of panic at their approach. It began to seem as if there were no law or order in the land. Society itself seemed demoralized, upset.

It was in such an atmosphere that political opinion altered, that parties dissolved and were reconstituted with many a novel purpose of reform. And yet the President moved in all matters which it fell to him to act upon with a vigor and initiative which made the years memorable. Strikes had been added to the other disturbances of the time. From April until June, 1894, a strike of the bituminous coal miners, two hundred thousand strong, threatened to embarrass the industries of the whole country. Many manufacturing establishments were obliged to close for lack of fuel.

COXEY BEING ESCORTED FROM THE CAPITOL

238

Some of the railways seized the coal which they were carrying as freight for use in feeding the fires of their locomotives. On the 11th of May a strike of the em-

GEORGE M. PULLMAN

ployees of the Pullman Car Company, of Chicago, began which presently became a very formidable affair. The strikers and their sympathizers mustered in dangerous numbers and made concerted effort to prevent the use of the cars of the Pullman Company by any of the railways running out of Chicago. Their violence seemed about to stop all traffic on the western roads, and Mr. Cleveland intervened. The governor of Illinois had not asked for his aid, had not even called out the militia of the State to maintain order and protect property,— sympathized, indeed, with the strikers and resented interference. Neither had the federal courts acted or asked for assistance in the execution of their writs. Mr. Cleveland deliberately took the initiative and assumed the responsibility, on the ground that the strikers were preventing the movement of the mails and blocking the course of interstate commerce, and that the carrying of the mails and the protection of commerce between the States were indisputable duties of the federal government. He ordered federal troops to the points of greatest violence and danger, and, when their mere presence and mere action as armed police did not suffice to check the mobs that aided the strikers, he issued a proclamation which practically declared the disturbed regions in a state of insurrection and threatened merciless action against all rioters as against public enemies. Order was restored and the law prevailed again.

In foreign affairs Mr. Cleveland exhibited the same firmness and decision, and had given the country a touch of his quality at the very outset of his term of office. One of his very first acts had been to withdraw from the docket of the Senate the treaty which Mr. Harrison had submitted to it for the annexation of the Hawaiian Islands to the United States. That treaty was the culminating transaction of a singular revolution. The Hawaiian Islands were subject to a sovereign queen whose power had been reduced by constitutional changes to the merely administrative function of exe-

THOMAS BRACKETT REED

cuting the laws passed by a representative chamber, to which, and not to herself, her ministers were responsible. Property and political power in the Islands had, by

LILIUOKALANI, QUEEN OF HAWAIIAN ISLANDS

processes which seemed to change the very character of the kingdom, come chiefly into the hands of foreigners; and in January, 1893, the queen determined to promulgate, upon her own sole authority, a new constitution which should deprive them of the suffrage and bring the legislature again under the control of the crown. The foreigners at Honolulu, the capital, chiefly Americans, at once bestirred themselves to defeat her purpose and get the government into their own hands, and the resident minister of the United States lent them his open aid. Marines and pieces of artillery were ordered on shore from a United States man-of-war lying in the harbor; under their protection a revolutionary provisional government was set up which thrust the queen aside "until terms of union with the United States had been negotiated and agreed upon"; and on the 16th of February, 1893, but a little more than two weeks before the expiration of his term as President, Mr. Harrison hurried a message to the Senate submitting an annexation treaty and recommending its ratification. Meantime, on the 9th of February, the minister of the United States at Honolulu, acting without instructions, had proclaimed a protectorate of the United States over the Islands.

On the 4th of March Mr. Cleveland assumed the presidency, and promptly withdrew the treaty. A commissioner was at once despatched to Hawaii to ascertain the full facts of the extraordinary transaction, and on the 18th of December, 1893, the President submitted his report to Congress, accompanied by a message in which he emphatically repudiated and condemned what the minister of the United States had taken it upon himself to do in the name of his government to put the revolution afoot. Had the displaced queen consented to a general amnesty and security of rights as the condition of her restoration, as Mr. Cleveland proposed, he would have undertaken to undo what the minister had done; but she would consent to no terms

whatever, and all things stood as they were, in the hands of the provisional government, self-constituted and born of revolution.

Eighteen months elapsed, the country saw the anx-

SETTING OUT FOR A DAY'S FISHING, HAWAII

ious summer of 1894, another winter brought the Treasury of the United States once again within sight of an exhaustion of its supply of gold, and then (July–December, 1895) a question of foreign policy came under the President's hand which might have embroiled two kindred nations in a great war. Once more the singular energy and decision of Mr. Cleveland's character were made evident, and the country was thrilled. For year after year through a long generation the English government had disputed with the government of Venezuela the western boundary line of British Guiana. From stage to stage of the controversy the line of the British claims had been pushed forward. Again and again, through one administration after another, the government of the United States had used its good offices to bring the controversy to a pacific and satisfactory conclusion. Ever since the famous declaration of Mr. Monroe, in 1823, it had been understood that the government of the United States would make it its business to see to it that no European power extended its dominion or acquired fresh territory in the Americas. It had not undertaken to maintain an actual formal protectorate over the South American states, but it did frankly undertake to act as their nearest friend in the settlement of controversies with European nations, and no President, whether Republican or Democratic, had hesitated since this critical dispute concerning the boundaries of British Guiana arose to urge its settlement upon terms favorable to Venezuela. The government at London had put settlement off, had frequently shifted its ground in the controversy, had always spoken of moderation, and yet had conceded nothing, had refused arbitration and yet had proposed no terms which it was possible for the Venezuelan government to accept. Endless irritation had led to no issue, and the matter seemed without term or solution when Mr. Cleveland uttered the word that concluded it. Earnest and repeated representations to Lord Salisbury having proved of no avail, Mr. Cleveland sent to Congress on the 17th of December, 1895, a message in which he set forth in unmistakable language what he believed to be the duty of the United States in the protection of Venezuelan rights. He had urged arbitration upon Lord Salisbury, as the most equitable, indeed the only possible, means of settling so old and so tangled a controversy;

THE MARQUIS OF SALISBURY

Lord Salisbury had declined arbitration and every settlement except that which conceded the full claims of England; it was necessary, therefore, the President declared, that the government of the United States should ascertain for itself the merits of the controversy, and, having reached a conclusion, insist upon its acceptance at whatever cost.

A thrill of intense excitement and enthusiasm shot through the country. Neither house of Congress was any longer of the President's party. The autumn elections of 1894 had replaced the heavy Democratic majority of 1892 by a Republican majority of one hundred and forty in the House of Representatives, and radical reversals of the majorities in the States had given the Senate also once more into the hands of the Republicans. But the houses forgot party differences in their eager and instant response to the President's Venezuelan message. Within three days after its receipt money had been voted for the commission of inquiry for which he asked, and all the world was apprised how ready the Congress was to support the President to the very utmost in his new and vigorous assertion of the Monroe doctrine. Thoughtful men knew very well how grievous a thing it would be to see the two kindred nations which stood so hopefully together at the front of the world's progress come to the awful grapple of war; no right-minded man in his senses wished to see so signal a catastrophe, least of all the President himself. He was a man of peace; but he deemed peace to be rooted in justice and feared it to be impossible with a nation which rejected the friendly offices of arbitration in a case like this that had arisen. He had in mind, too, the peculiar relations which the government over which he presided had always borne to the states of South America in respect of their dealings with the nations of Europe, and knew that he could not in fidelity relax the rigor of the principle upon which it had these seventy years been its avowed policy to act. It was that, his assertion of the Monroe doctrine in a new aspect, with a new dignity, even if with a new rigor, that caught

247

the almost passionate enthusiasm of the country, and made war unnecessary. Lord Salisbury yielded; the dispute was submitted to arbitration; and Mr. Cleveland had a great triumph. He had exposed a hidden question to the public opinion of two nations, and that opinion had supported him and rebuked Lord Salisbury.

Mr. Cleveland pushed his belief in arbitration far beyond the individual instance. In the spring of 1895, Mr. Gresham, then Secretary of State, had suggested to Her Majesty's government a general treaty of arbitration in which the two governments should pledge themselves to submit all serious matters of dispute that might arise between them to settlement by an impartial outside tribunal; the sudden heat of the Venezuelan controversy quickened the desire on both sides of the water to carry the plan into execution; and on the 11th of January, 1897, the President had the satisfaction of seeing such a treaty completed and signed. But the Senate rejected it. Mr. Cleveland's term of office came to an end within two months after the exchange of signatures, and a Republican President succeeded him while the treaty pended. The new President urged the treaty upon the Senate as he had urged it, but it was rejected, notwithstanding. The Senate would not bind the government to submit its interests in all cases to the decisions of an outside tribunal, and the careful diplomatic work of two governments went for nothing.

Those closing days of the Democratic administration were darkened by perplexities of foreign policy essentially more serious and difficult to handle than any that were likely to arise between the governments of the United States and Great Britain. The difficulties of Spanish rule in Cuba were growing intolerable. Sharp insurrection had broken forth there in the spring of 1895. It was but seventeen years since

WALTER QUINTON GRESHAM

the last uprising in the island, which had lasted the ten years 1868–1878, and which had been brought to a conclusion only by promises of radical reform in the

Spanish administration. Those promises had not been kept. The reforms instituted had proved delusive. The island was taxed to the uttermost farthing for the support of the army and navy and of the host of Spanish officials who throve as placemen in the innumerable offices of administration. The suffrage that had been granted the native inhabitants and the privileges of self-government which had been accorded them were effectually offset by laws which really put their affairs at the disposal of the Captain General who was their governor; and men who were not within the circles of official influence complained that they could get no privilege, enforce no right, even, which they did not pay for in hard cash. A mere petty fraction of the intolerable taxes they paid was expended upon the public works of the island itself. There seemed no way of reform except by revolution, and no hope even in revolution unless its object were absolute independence. The Spanish government met the insurrection with savage measures of suppression. In January, 1896, Don Valeriano Weyler was made governor and Captain General of the island, and proceeded to take measures of repression which shocked the humane sense of all civilized peoples looking on. Finding that it made no end of resistance merely to harry the country with its fastnesses of forest, swamp, and mountain, he began to destroy every village and habitation of the insurrectionary districts and to drive the women and children who inhabited them into camps of "concentration," where they might be kept under guard and surveillance and held off from giving succor or intelligence to the insurgents, in order that the country might be empty and without homely shelter; and he did not take the precautions of mere prudence and mercy which were necessary to keep fatal diseases and pitiful starvation out of the camps, but let the poor creatures huddled there live for the most part as they could.

DON VALERIANO WEYLER

Opinion moved very uneasily in the United States at sight of such things and the President had no mind to ignore them. No one could pretend that it was, or that it ought to be, a thing indifferent to the United States to have chronic rebellion and suffering thus perpetuated from year to year in a populous island lying at their very doors, to which their people were closely bound by trade and all the intimate intercourse of neighbors. Fatal fevers had again and again crossed the narrow waters out of Cuba to the southern ports of the United States because the Spaniards would not look to the proper sanitation of the great towns which lay by the island's harbors, and these distempers of revolution seemed as ill to take the wind of as the fevers themselves. Mr. Cleveland spoke very gravely in his annual message of December, 1896, of the necessity of bringing affairs in Cuba to a final pacification and adjustment. "It cannot be reasonably assumed," he said, "that the hitherto expectant attitude of the United States will be indefinitely maintained. While we are anxious to accord all due respect to the sovereignty of Spain, we cannot view the pending conflict in all its features and properly apprehend our inevitably close relations to it, and its possible results, without considering that by the course of events we may be drawn into such an unusual and unprecedented condition as will fix a limit to our patient waiting for Spain to end the contest, either alone and in her own way, or with our friendly co-operation." The phrases were guarded but the meaning was plain. Spain must come to some terms of accommodation with her Cuban subjects or the United States must intervene. Every private effort of negotiation had been made to bring peace and concession; the government's words of protest began now to be spoken aloud and before the world.

It was not yet time to act, and the guidance of action, should action become necessary, must fall to other men. The end of Mr. Cleveland's anxious term was at hand. He left his great office as if with a sense of relief.

His party had turned away from him. For two years he had carried the burdens of the government alone. The Republican houses elected in 1894 would do nothing more to make his tasks possible than the Democratic houses had done. Again and again he had asked their assistance in the relief of the Treasury, to protect the gold reserve and steady the business of the country. Plan after plan had been matured by the Secretary of the Treasury, Mr. Carlisle, and the President had sought by every possible means to serve thoughtful opinion and right purposes of reform with regard to the finances. But Congress would accept nothing that he proposed. He had been left to come to what agreements he could with the great bankers of Wall Street for the protection and replenishment of the gold reserve, they alone being able, without legislation, to assist him in that matter. He was obliged to bargain with them like any other borrower to obtain the gold the Treasury needed and control the draughts the banks in their turn made upon it. The strain of the responsibility had been grievous to bear : the whole fabric of credit seemed to rest upon the foundations which he kept so laboriously in repair, and the months seemed very long while the doubtful work went on. When the end came he felt that he had earned his rest and quiet retirement.

The elections of 1896 had shown, in a fashion the country was not likely to forget, the volcanic forces which had been kept but just beneath the surface while he was President. The issue which had dominated all the rest was the question of the coinage. But that question did not stand alone. It seemed, indeed, but a single item in the agitated thought of the time. Opinion everywhere seemed to have broken from its old moorings. There had been real distress in the country, long continued, hopeless, as if the springs of wealth and prosperity were dried up. The distress was most marked and apparently most hopeless in the great agricultural areas of the South and West. The prices of agricultural products had fallen so low that universal bankruptcy seemed to the farmers to be but a little way off. There was a marked depression in all kinds of business, as if enterprise were out of heart and money nowhere to be had except among a few great capitalists in Wall Street. Men's minds anxiously sought the cause, and each man reasoned upon it in the light of his own observation and experience, taking his views of matters which lay beyond his own life from the politicians who spoke most plausibly of public affairs. Every established relationship of law and of society fell under question. Did not the law too much favor the combinations of capital by which small dealers and producers were shut out of the markets? Were the courts not on the side of those who had privilege, and against those who had none? Were not the railways the real masters of the producer everywhere, able to make or to unmake him by their charges and discriminations? Was not money scarce because the government would issue none that was not kept to the standard of gold, itself too scarce, too artificially costly to be made the universal medium of exchange?

The money question was but one of the innumerable questions that crowded into men's minds in that time of agitation, but it seemed the question which lay at the centre of all the rest, and it more than any other gathered passion about it. Men do not think with cool detachment about the financial questions which touch their very means of subsistence. They were easily persuaded that money would be more plentiful, for the individual as for the nation, if scarce gold were abandoned as the exclusive standard of value and abundant silver substituted, so that there should be metal currency enough for all; and they were easily beguiled to dream what a blessed age should come when the thing should have been done. They were not studious of the laws of value. They knew that the resources of the country were abundant, that its prosperity came from its own skill and its own wealth of rich material, and that it was getting a certain predominance in the markets of the world. They could not see why it should not be sufficient unto itself, why its standards of value should not be its own, irrespective of the practice of other countries, why its credit should be affected by the basis upon which the currency of other countries rested, or why international trade should dominate its domestic transactions. All the world had in fact become at last a single commercial community. No nation, least of all a nation which lived by trade and manufacture, could stand aloof and insist that an ounce of gold should not be considered more valuable than sixteen ounces of silver when mere fact was against it and the free law of supply and demand worked its will despite the statutes of legislatures. But very few men who did not actually handle the trade of the world saw the inexorable laws of value as they existed in fact. It went naturally with the vast extent of the continent that most men were shut off from a sight of the international forces which governed their economic interests, and a very passion of belief had got abroad that all the economic stagnation of the times could be relieved by the

255

free coinage of both gold and silver at the ratio of sixteen to one.

It was no ordinary political opinion such as might in any election year come forward to dominate men's votes. It set men's minds on fire, filled them with an eager ardor like that of religious conviction, impelled them to break old associations and seek new comradeships in affairs. Party lines were cut athwart. The Republicans no doubt had their chief strength in the central and eastern States of the Union, where trade and manufacture moved strongest and men were most apt to understand the wide foundations of their business; the Democrats drew their support, rather, from the South and West, where disturbing changes of opinion had long been in progress and where radical programmes of relief were most apt to be looked upon with favor; and yet it was by no means certain that these new opinions upon the money question had not touched Republican voters too deeply to make it prudent for their leaders to take high ground of opposition against them. An extraordinary campaign of propaganda had been begun before the year of the presidential election came on. The advocates of the free coinage of silver were early afoot, with the ardor and irresistible zeal of veritable crusaders, to overcome dissent in both parties alike and force the country to a common view. A great national conference of silver advocates had been convened at Washington in March, 1895, and had marked the beginning of an organized movement which was carried forward with extraordinary vigor and effect, to control the action of the party conventions. As the year of the elections lengthened towards summer State after State in the South and West declared unequivocally for free coinage, and conservative men everywhere waited with a deep uneasiness to see what the leaders of the national parties would do.

The Republican convention met first, and in it the advocates of the gold standard won. The convention declared itself "unalterably opposed to every measure calculated to debase our currency or impair the credit of our country, and therefore opposed to the free coinage of silver except by international agreement with the leading commercial nations of the world." Its choice of a candidate for the presidency was not quite so definite an evidence of its purpose with regard to the currency as the words of its platform. It nominated Mr. William McKinley, recently governor of Ohio, and known to all the country for his long service in the House of Representatives, especially as chairman of the Committee of Ways and Means which had formulated the tariff of 1890 against which the Democrats had won at the polls in 1892. Mr. McKinley had more than once spoken and voted on the silver question, and had not shown himself unwilling to consider very seriously the claims of the advocates of the cheaper metal as a standard of value. They had accounted him, if not a friend, at least no determined opponent, at any rate of some of the measures upon which they had set their hearts. But there was no doubt of his great credit with his party as a man and a leader, and his explicit acquiescence in the principles of the platform upon which he had been nominated satisfied the country of his good faith and conservative purpose. The issue was definitively made up.

Three weeks later the Democratic convention demanded "the free and unlimited coinage of both gold and silver at the present legal ratio of sixteen to one, without waiting for the aid or consent of any other nation," and nominated Mr. William Jennings Bryan, of Nebraska, for the presidency. It acted with singular excitement and swung sharply away from conservative influences. It denounced what Mr. Cleveland had done to save the gold reserve and to check the riots at Chicago as hotly as any Republican policy; spoke of the decisions of the Supreme Court of the United States against the income tax as if it advocated a change in the very character of the court, should power come to the party it represented; and uttered radical doctrines of reform which sounded like sentences taken from the platforms of the People's party. Its nomination for the presidency was significant of its temper and excitement. Mr. Bland, of Missouri, one of the older leaders of the party, and a man whose name all the country knew to stand for the advanced doctrines of free coinage, had at first led in the balloting. Mr. Bryan, though he had been a member of Congress and had spoken in the House upon the coinage question, had made no place of leadership for himself hitherto, was unknown to the country at large and even to the great mass of his fellow partisans, and had come to the convention with the delegation from Nebraska unheralded, unremarked. A single speech made from the platform of the convention had won him the nomination, a speech wrought, not of argument, but of fire, and uttered in the full tones of a voice which rang clear and passionate in the authentic key of the assembly's own mood of vehemence and revolt. It was a thing for thoughtful men to note how a mere stroke of telling declamation might make an unknown, untested man the nominee of

WILLIAM JENNINGS BRYAN

a great party for the highest office in the land, a popular assembly being the instrument of choice.

The People's party also accepted Mr. Bryan as its candidate. It uttered in its platform some radical purposes which the new Democratic leaders had not adopted, but it did not require its candidate himself to accept them. It recognized the coinage issue as the chief question of the moment, and was willing that he should be its spokesman in that. Parties were singularly confused and broken. Two weeks after the Democratic convention a considerable body of Republicans, advocates of the free coinage of silver, rejected in the counsels of their own party, assembled in convention at St. Louis, calling themselves the National Silver party, and there in their turn endorsed the candidacy and the views of Mr. Bryan. Early in September an influential body of men out of the Democratic ranks came together in convention at Indianapolis, calling themselves the National Democratic party, and formulated once more what conservative men believed to be the true traditional doctrines of the Democratic party upon questions of taxation, revenue, and coinage. Men of strong party faith hardly knew which way to turn. The great deep seemed broken up, old landmarks swept away, parties merged, confused, dispersed. Only the Republican party preserved its full historical identity. Its opponents were united in novel, uncertain, motley assembly; it was at least compact and definite.

The money issue seemed the only issue of the campaign. Party orators spoke often of other things, but upon that they grappled in close, stubborn, impassioned argument. The country had never seen such a struggle to rule opinion. Such excitement, such a stirring of

the moral and intellectual forces of the country, on the
one side as if to regenerate society, on the other as if
to save it from disruption, had never before marked
a political campaign. The election even of 1860 had
been preceded by no such fever of agitation. The Democrats and their allies had the dramatic advantage. Their
candidate made a gallant figure wherever he moved, and
went up and down the country, as no presidential candidate before him had ever done, to give the people his
own striking version of the doctrines he preached. To
the excited crowds which pressed about him he seemed
a sort of knight errant going about to redress the wrongs
of a nation. There could be no mistaking his earnest-
ness or his conviction or the deep power of the motives
to which he appealed. His gifts were those of the practised orator, his qualities those of the genuine man of
the people. His strong, musical voice carried his message to the utmost limits of any throng, and rang in a
tone which warmed men's blood. There could be no
doubting the forces of conviction which lay back of him.
Very likely there were many charlatans in the convention
which nominated him, and men who acted upon mere expediency, but the crowding ranks in that hall had been
made up for the most part of men who deeply believed
every word of the radical programme they put forth;
and the great throngs out-of-doors who cheered the sentences of that platform with full-throated ardor cheered
because they also believed. No one could deny that
the country had fallen upon evil times, that the poor
man found it harder than ever to live, and that many a
law needed to be looked into which put the poor at a disadvantage. The country teemed with men who found
themselves handicapped in all they tried to do,—they

could but conjecture why. It was no new thing that multitudes, and multitudes of sensible men at that, should think that the remedy lay in making new laws of coinage and exchange. The battle was to be won by argument, not by ridicule or terror or mere stubbornness of vested interest.

It was won by argument. The country had never seen such a flood of pamphlets, such a rush of every man who could speak to the platform, of every man who could write into the columns of the newspapers and the pages of the magazines. It was in the last analysis a contest between the radical and the conservative forces of the country, and the conservative forces won. The election day, the 3d of November, saw more than fourteen million votes cast, and of these more than six and a half million were cast for Mr. Bryan. Mr. McKinley received 7,111,607. Every State north of the Ohio and the Potomac and east of the Mississippi gave its electoral votes to the Republican candidate, some of them, like New York and New Jersey, by unprecedented majorities. West of the Mississippi the Republicans carried Minnesota, Iowa, North Dakota, Oregon, and California, and south of the Ohio and Potomac West Virginia and Kentucky. Even in North Carolina and Tennessee the Republican vote leaped up in significant strength. Nowhere did the tide of Democratic votes run as the tide of Republican votes ran in the States where opinion rallied strong to maintain the established foundations of business. Republican majorities were returned again, also, to both houses of Congress; and no one could doubt the verdict of the country.

It was a singular thing how the excitement subsided

when the sharp contest was over and the result known. Never before, perhaps, had there been occasion to witness so noteworthy an illustration of the peaceable fruits of untrammelled self-government, the cheerful, immediate, hearty acquiescence of a self-governing people in the processes of its own political life. Not a tone of revolt was to be heard. The defeated party was content to await another election and abide by the slow processes of argument and conviction, and affairs went forward almost as if with a sense of relief on both sides that the fight had been fought out and settled. Business took heart again. Whatever might be said for or against the free coinage of the two money metals at a ratio which was not the actual ratio of their real relative values, definite assurance as to the policy to be pursued was an indispensable prerequisite to the confident carrying forward of business enterprises; and the verdict of the country had at last been given so decisively that capitalists need, it seemed, have no uneasy misgivings even with regard to the next election, when another four years should have gone by.

And yet the air had not cleared entirely; the task of the party now restored to full power was not simplified by the mere vote of the people. Questions of internal war and peace were, indeed, past, forgotten. In March, 1896, the houses, Republican though they were, had taken from the statute book the only fragment that remained of confederate disabilities, enacting "That section twelve hundred and eighteen of the Revised Statutes of the United States, as amended by chapter forty-six of the laws of 1884, which section is as follows: 'No person who held a commission in the Army or Navy of the United States at the beginning of the late rebellion, and afterwards served in any capacity in the military, naval, or civil service of the so-called Confederate States, or of either of the States in insurrection during the late rebellion, shall be appointed to any position in the Army or Navy of the United States,' be, and the same is hereby, repealed." It was the final "Act of Oblivion"; affairs would never again turn back to that day of bitterness and strife. It might be that even the deep agitation with regard to the money question was quieted. But no one could think that the influences which had stirred that troublesome question to such a heat had been set aside by the mere suffrages of the voters.

Obviously the business world, the whole world of industry, was in process of revolution. America, in particular, had come to the crisis and turning point of her development. Until now she had been struggling to release and organize her resources, to win her true economic place in the world. Hitherto she had been always a debtor nation, her instruments of industry making and to be made, her means of transportation, the vast systems of steel highways which were to connect her fields and factories with the markets of the world, as yet only in course of construction. At the close of the civil war there were but thirty-five thousand miles of railway upon all the vast spaces of the continent; there were one hundred and fifty thousand more to add before its products and manufactures could be handled freely in the world's exchanges, and for that vast increase foreign as well as domestic capital had to be borrowed by the hundreds of millions. Except what her fields produced, the country had as yet but little with which to pay the interest and the capital of her debts:

William McKinley

her fields were in some sense the granary of the world. As agricultural prices fell it required more and more food stuffs to pay her balances. In those fatal years of depression, 1893–1896, when business threatened to stand still because of the state of the currency and the crops fetched little more than would pay for their carriage, it was necessary to pay huge foreign balances in coin, and $87,000,000 in gold had had to be shipped over sea to the country's creditors in a single twelvemonth (1893). It was that extraordinary drain that made Mr. Cleveland's task next to impossible, to keep the Treasury reserve unexhausted and yet sustain the currency with gold payments. Not until the very year 1897, when the new Republican administration came in, did the crisis seem to be past. The country had at last built its railway and manufacturing systems up, had at last got ready to come out of its debts, command foreign markets with something more than its food stuffs, and make for itself a place of mastery. The turning point seemed to be marked by a notable transaction which took place the very month Mr. McKinley was inaugurated. In March, 1897, a great consolidation of iron-mining properties, foundries, steel mills, railroads, and steamship lines was effected which brought the country's chief supplies of iron, its chief steel producing plants, and its chief means of transporting steel products to the markets of the continent and of the world under a single organization and management, and reduced the cost of steel to a figure which put American steel factories beyond fear of competition. Steel had become the structural stuff of the modern world. Commanding its manufacture, America might command the economic fortunes of the world.

It was this new aspect of industry that disclosed the problems Republican and Democratic statesmen were to face for the coming generation. The concentration of capital was no new thing; but the new scale upon which it now began to be effected made it seem a thing novel and unexpected. The control now of this industry and again of that by small groups of capitalists, the growth of monopolies, the union of producers in each line of manufacture for the purpose of regulating prices to their own liking and profit, had been familiar circumstances, familiar signs of the times, these twenty years. The farmers had seen them and had formed their granges, their Alliances, their People's party to protect their own interests, by combination and political agitation, against the huge corporate powers that seemed to be gathering for the conquest of fortune. The industrial workingmen had seen them and had widened their organizations to meet the threat of subjection. The great strikes which followed one another, summer by summer, with such significant regularity were but the reflex of what was taking place in Wall Street, where huge combinations of capital were being arranged; at the manufacturing centres of the country, where the interests of producers were being pooled; at railway centres, where great systems of transportation were being drawn together under a single management. Mines, factories, railways, steamships were now, it appeared, to be brought into one corporate union as a single business. It was the culmination of the process, and seemed to put a new face on all that had gone before, on all that was to follow.

No wonder thoughtful men, as well as mere labor agitators, grew uneasy and looked about them to see

what control the law could exercise. No doubt there
was risk of deeply serious consequence in these vast
aggregations of capital, these combinations of all the
processes of a great industry in the hands of a single
"Trust." No doubt they did give to a few men a control
over the economic life of the country which they might
abuse to the undoing of millions of men, it might even
be to the permanent demoralization of society itself
and of the government which was the instrument of
society in the conduct of its united interests. The
programmes of socialists and extremists proposed a
remedy which was but a completion of the process: the
virtual control of all industry and of all the means of
transportation by the government itself. The leaders
of the People's party, though they professed no social-
istic doctrine, demanded government ownership of the
railway and telegraph lines of the country, and their
expressed desire with regard to the control of "Trusts"
smacked of the extremest purposes of experiment in
the field of legislation. The Interstate Commerce Act
had been a beginning, a very conservative beginning,
in the carrying out of what they wished to see undertaken. Neither the leaders of the Republican party
nor the leaders of the Democratic party felt that such
impulses of reform, such counsels of restriction could
be entirely ignored; but neither party saw as yet the
prudent and practicable lines of action. It would not
do to check the processes which were adding so enormously to the economy and efficiency of the nation's
productive work and promising to give her now at last
that first place in wealth and power in the world which
every son who loved her had predicted she should some
day have; and yet it would not do to leave the economic

liberty of the individual or the freedom and self-respect of the workingman unprotected.

The first steps taken by the new administration for the relief of the economic situation were not of the new order, but of the old. Mr. McKinley at once summoned Congress to meet in extraordinary session on the 15th of March, in order to provide the government with additional revenue. He interpreted the elections which had brought him into office to mean that the country desired not only to avoid the free coinage of silver but also to return to the protective system of duties exemplified in the tariff of 1890. The Ways and Means Committee of the House had prepared a tariff bill during the last session, while they waited for the change of administration. Upon the convening of Congress in extraordinary session, Mr. Dingley, their chairman, reported it at once, and by the end of the month it had passed the House and been sent to the Senate. It lingered close upon four months in the Senate and in the conference committee which sat to adjust the differences between the two houses; and when it became law, on the 24th of July, contained no systematic scheme of taxation at all, but merely a miscellany of taxes on the innumerable imports which were to be expected every year out of foreign ports. Its rates, upon the average, rose even above those of 1890. Some articles, like raw hides, which had been on the free list for a quarter of a century, were again subjected to duty; the sugar men again got what they desired; some duties, like that on flax, were imposed to please the farmers; some, like that on lead and lead ores, to placate the senators who were of the silver interest of the western mining country. Here and there, noticeably in the metal schedules, the rates were left as they had stood since 1894; the duty on steel rails was even slightly reduced, as if the great steel industry at least were counted on to take care of itself. The net result was a return to the highest principles of protection, or, if no principle could be discovered in the Act, at least to its most extreme practices. A year later (June 18, 1898) an Act was passed which created an Industrial Commission whose function it was to be to collate information and to consider and recommend legislation with regard to the many complicated problems presented by labor, agriculture, and the industrial use of capital. An Act had preceded it by some two weeks (June 1, 1898) which made provision for the arbitration of labor disputes between common carriers and their employees engaged in interstate commerce, to avoid, if possible, the difficulties which Mr. Cleveland had been obliged to settle by the use of federal troops. But as yet protective tariffs, inquiry into economic conditions, and provision for arbitration were all that the leaders of the houses had to offer towards the solution of the questions out of which the silver agitation had sprung.

The attention of the country was for the time being drawn off to other things. There had come a day, the day to which Mr. Cleveland had looked forward and of whose approach he had warned the government of Spain, when the patience of the country with regard to the situation in Cuba was exhausted. Much as the pitiful process of subjugation still dragged, moving as was the spectacle of a fair country devastated to bring, not healing peace, but mere submission, opinion might for a little while longer have been held off from dangerous heat in the matter had not a sudden, startling incident, tragical and full of every element calculated to stir passion, sent a final thrill of excitement through the country. On the evening of the 14th of February, 1898, Saint Valentine's Day, the United States battle-ship *Maine*, lying in Havana harbor upon a visit of courtesy, was blown to pieces, and two of her officers, two hundred and fifty-eight of her crew, killed upon the instant. The most careful investigation failed to disclose the origin of the explosion; but an examination of the twisted wreck made it plain that it had come from no accident within the ship itself. The explosives which had destroyed her had lain beneath her at the bottom of the harbor where she had her anchorage. Within two months Spain and the United States were at war,—not because a vessel of the American navy had been destroyed in a port of Spain, but because opinion leaped upon the provocation of that tragic incident from quiet inquiry to hot impatience with regard to all the ugly Cuban business. There was no evidence whatever that any one connected with the exercise of Spanish authority in Cuba had had so much as guilty knowledge of the plans made to destroy the *Maine;* but that unhappy explosion had changed the whole air of opinion the country through.

There was no calculating the forces of excitement that were abroad; there was no determining their origin or their real power. No doubt influences were at work which did not wait upon opinion, which made opinion their covert merely and means of justification. Sensational newspapers exaggerated every phase of the disturbing incidents of the time, to make news and increase their sales; men who saw personal gain in store for them amidst the risks of war bestirred themselves to make

THE UNITED STATES BATTLESHIP MAINE AT ANCHOR IN HAVANA HARBOR

interest against Spain in the houses at Washington;
politicians were quick to say and do what they hoped
would enhance their credit and the influence of their
party with the country; personal ambitions were not
neglected in the eagerness of Congress to make some
stroke in behalf of Cuba and for the aggrandizement
of the power of the United States in the West Indies.
Mr. McKinley had no such mastery as could hold the
impulses of members in check. He had spent fourteen
years on the floor of the House of Representatives.
His point of view with regard to the exercise of his constitutional powers was not that which Mr. Cleveland had
exemplified. He did not act as an independent, originative force in the determination of policy, but rather as a
power intimately associated with the law-making branch
of the government. He was not only sensitive to opinion out-of-doors but also to the intimations of purpose
which came to him from the leaders of the houses. The
fine quality of the man was evident to all who approached
him: his sense of duty, his devotion to the principles
which he conceived to be the principles of right action,
his kindliness, his modesty, his Christian self-forget-
fulness. His unfailing tact seemed to take the sting
from the sharpest differences of opinion or of purpose
upon whatever matter, and men did not draw off from
him because he refused them what they asked or dis-
sented from them in what they thought. But he seemed
to stand like a leader who received his ideas, not from
his own individual examination of affairs or the action
of his own originative powers upon the subject matter
of public policy, but from the men about him whom
he most trusted, from the subtle airs of opinion abroad
out-of-doors, from those who brought him the counsels

of Congress and the news of events. There was no impression of weakness to be got in dealing with him, but an impression of sober sensibility, rather, and of sanguine confidence in the movements of opinion.

He had diligently pressed upon the Spanish government every argument for peace with its Cuban subjects, for accommodation, for friendly intervention by the United States, for reform and concession in the government of the island that diplomatic usage and international courtesy permitted, and yet the end of the Cuban trouble seemed no nearer than before. He quickened his pace in the business as he saw opinion advance and the houses grow impatient,—quickened it very much when the destruction of the *Maine* put a touch of fever into men's thoughts. Congress was the war-making power: it very soon became evident that it could not much longer be restrained from radical action. Distressing reports poured in every day of the sufferings of the Cuban people, especially in the camps of concentration. The island was nearby: news came fresh from the very scenes of war and desolation. Members of Congress themselves visited the concentration camps and the parts of the island where the insurrection had its chief seats, and told from their places on the floor what they had seen and heard. The President wished to keep the reins in his own hands, but feared every week to see the restive houses break from his control. Fast as negotiation had moved on the heels of the excitement that followed that fatal explosion in Havana harbor it had not moved fast enough to please the impatient spirits who pressed the leaders of Congress for action. Towards the last it had begun to look as if the Spanish government were ready, rather than let the war feeling in the United States put things beyond all possibility of a peaceful solution, to make very substantial concessions to the Cuban insurgents and bring the troubles of the island to an end. But Mr. McKinley doubted the good faith of the concessions offered, found them guarded by proposed processes of execution which might take perilously long in the carrying out, believed that opinion in the country would not justify him in taking any further risks of disappointment, and made a sudden end of negotiation. On the 11th of April, 1898, he asked Congress for authority to put an end to the hostilities in Cuba, and on the 18th Congress declared the Cuban people free and independent and authorized the President to use the military and naval forces of the United States to compel the government of Spain to relinquish its authority and government in the island. The Spanish minister at Washington of course asked for his passports, all diplomatic relations between the two governments were broken off, and on the 25th of April formal declaration of war was made. The resolutions agreed to by the houses in authorizing the President to drive Spain from the island had concluded with this solemn statement of the purposes of the United States: "The United States hereby disclaims any disposition or intention to exercise sovereignty, jurisdiction, or control over said island, except for the pacification thereof, and asserts its determination when that is accomplished to leave the government and control of the island to its people." Intervention had come, not for the material aggrandizement of the United States, but for the assertion of the right of the government to succor those who seemed hopelessly oppressed, to recover the peace and order of its coasts, to free its trade from the

WEST IN

BORMAY & CO., N.Y.

trammels put upon it by a war to which there seemed no end, to quiet the thoughts of its own people in order that they might turn again without distraction to their own affairs.

It was a war of impulse, as any one might see who noted how unprepared the country was for what it had suddenly undertaken. The regular army of the United States numbered but 28,000, officers and men. It fell to volunteers as much as to regular troops to assume the burdens of the field, as in the war for the Union and the war against Mexico fifty years ago. The regular army was increased to more than 42,000 before the month of May was out; but the new men were, of course, mere recruits, and the volunteers mustered faster than the regulars. Before the end of May, in response to the proclamations of the President, more than 118,000 men and six thousand officers had been mustered into the volunteer service, chiefly from the militia of the States, and had been equipped and distributed among the various camps of preparation in which they were to be made ready and await their orders. Congress authorized the increase of the regular army to 65,000 men, and by the close of August more than 56,000 had been mustered in. The volunteer forces had by that time grown to 216,256, men crowding into the ranks from every quarter of the country. It was noted how eagerly the southerners pressed forward for service. Elderly men who had been officers in the armies of the southern Confederacy asked for commands, and got them, under the Act of indemnity passed but two years before. The country was thrilled with a new sense of union and of enthusiasm for a common cause. There was no longer any thought of differences between section and section

when the flag was in the field. Those days together
in camp and battle set the war between the States another full generation back, into a past now left at last
for historians, not politicians, to take care of.

Before the first season of enthusiasm had gone by
the war was over. It was ended before the ranks were
full. July was not out before the American troops had
had their will in Cuba and Porto Rico, and Spain had
proposed terms of peace. By the middle of August
Manila, in the far Philippines, had been taken; no
Spanish force anywhere resisted the arms of the United
States; only the full terms of peace remained to be agreed
upon. The navy of the United States had been the
first to give the Spaniard a taste of its quality. There
had been no question of making it ready for war. It
was outnumbered by many of the great navies of the
world, but its officers were professional experts trained
to proficiency by as thorough a schooling and experience
in arms as if war were always at hand; and their ships
were of the most modern type and equipment, built where
the best steel and the best machinists of the world were
to be had. Every stroke that they made told. On the
1st of May, in the grey of the early morning, Commodore
Dewey, commanding the squadron of the United States
in eastern waters, attacked the Spanish fleet in the
bay of Manila, the capital city of the Philippines,
and by noon had utterly destroyed it, his own fleet suffering little damage, and without the loss of a single
life on his ships. He had entered the great bay under
cover of the preceding night, steaming past the batteries
which stood guard there upon Corregidor Island and
through the long channels where he had been told tor-
pedoes had been set, as he had steamed when a boy with

CITY OF SAN JUAN, PORTO RICO

Commodore Farragut past the batteries and the torpe-does at the mouths of the Mississippi. The force of his guns was greater than that of the inferior pieces on the Spanish ships, and but few of their shots took effect; the marksmanship of his gunners made their fire precise and terrible; he led his ships slowly back and forth along the line of the Spaniards' anchorage until the whole fleet he had been bidden destroy lay sunken, burn-ing, and abandoned. That done, the city, with its old-fashioned walls and ancient defences, was at his mercy. It had been a gallant exploit gallantly undertaken, against unknown risks and dangers which he could only guess, against a force whose real power and equip-ment were not known, and executed with a business-like thoroughness which caught the imagination of every man who loved thoroughbred service and daring. Congress sent the Commodore increase of rank with its thanks, and troops were hurried aboard the transports at San Francisco to act with him in the capture and occupation of Manila.

The tasks of the fleets mustered to invest the Cuban ports and convey the troops of the United States to their attack upon the island were by no means so simple. The coasts of the long island had many ports; it was presently known that a Spanish squadron of four ar-mored cruisers and three torpedo-boat destroyers, un-der Admiral Pascual Cervera, had left the Cape Verde Islands for the West Indies; it was possible to do little more than guess what port they would make for. There were not vessels enough to watch all the coasts of Cuba and Porto Rico. It might be that the Spanish admiral would first make some demonstration against a port of the United States, and it gave the authorities at Washington and all who thought upon the matter no small concern to think how little had been done to supply the open coast of the continent with adequate defences. As it turned out, Admiral Cervera ran straight into

PASCUAL CERVERA

Santiago de Cuba, the southern port of the island, which lay nearest the open seas by which he had approached. The Carribean Sea was wide; the American commanders got word first that he had touched at Martinique, then that he had touched at Curaçoa, close by the Gulf

279

of Venezuela; there was no making his course out from that, and he slipped unobserved into Santiago while the American commander-in-chief searched for him off the harbors of Porto Rico. At Santiago he lay almost a full fortnight before his whereabouts was discovered by the anxious American sailors. High hills shut the closed harbor in, and a narrow, winding channel served it for entrance; no ship at sea, no one who did not stand upon the very hills that overlooked the harbor, could discover what craft lay within the hidden bay. But by the 29th of May a flying squadron of the American fleet, under Commodore Schley, had established a blockade of the port, reasonably assured that the Spanish squadron was within, and by the 1st of June acting Rear Admiral Sampson, the commander-in-chief, had arrived, to add his heavier ships to the blockading force and take command.

The whereabouts of the Spanish fleet determined the point of attack for the army as well as for the men-of-war. General Shafter, commanding the troops assembled at Tampa, in Florida, was ordered to take some sixteen thousand men under convoy to Santiago, 14,000 regulars and 2,500 volunteers, in order that the town with its garrison and the fleet lying in its bay might be taken together, by the joint action of the land and naval forces. There were not sufficient railway facilities for sending the troops to their place of embarkation; there were not harbor facilities enough for the difficult work of embarking the troops where the transports lay; no one in chief command seemed ever to have seriously studied the handling of men and stores upon the great scale; there was infinite delay and confusion and blundering before the expedition was ready to sail. It took an entire week to effect the embarkation, and the ships were held yet another week at their anchorage after the troops were aboard before they finally put to sea, because

WILLIAM R. SHAFTER

of false rumors of Spanish cruisers on the coasts they were to approach. But by the 14th of June they were under weigh, and by the morning of the 20th were off the coasts where they were to be put ashore. On the 22d,

281

23d, and 24th they were landed at Daiquiri and Siboney, some twelve to fifteen miles east of the town of Santiago, and their painful work began. The country through which they had to pass was broken into abrupt and difficult hills; the roads were hardly more than bridle paths, and ran through thick tangles of tropical undergrowth. The flooding rains of the region were likely at any time to render them impassable and cut the troops off as they advanced alike from further movement upon their objective and from communication with their base of supplies at the rear where the transports lay. The distempers of the unfamiliar climate took immediate hold upon them, and sapped their strength. There were not surgeons or nurses or medical stores enough, and the lack of organized and efficient means and methods of transportation worked an injury there worse by far than it had worked at Tampa. At Tampa the blundering and mismanagement had been stupid, irritating; here they were deeply tragical. It was pitiful what rank and file alike had to endure, with stores unpacked, untouched at the rear, and medicines left where they could be of no service. But pluck and intelligence carried the regiments forward to the overcoming of difficulties and the winning of battles there as they had carried the men like them who went with General Scott to the conquest of Mexico fifty years before. Division commanders proved more efficient and resourceful than their superiors in command; privates knew their duty without orders, shifted for themselves in camp, at mess, and on the march like men who did not need to be cared for, endured what came to them without murmur or discouragement, and moved like those who act confidently without command, carried forward

by their own wits and courage and habits of concerted action.

By the morning of the 1st of July the decisive movements of the attack were planned and begun and by the evening of that day an advantage had been gained which made it certain what the end must be. The town of El Caney and the strong hill of San Juan had been stormed and taken, the one commanding the road to Guantanamo, by which the garrison of the city might expect succor, and whence they could threaten the flank of any force that moved direct upon Santiago, the other commanding the straight approaches to the city itself. El Caney lay in a position of natural strength and was protected by strong block houses, a stone fort, a stone church, itself a sort of fort loopholed for rifles, and long lines of trenches cut in the solid rock. The hill of San Juan stood steep and guarded, crowned with a block fort set about with a maze of barbed wire entanglements. The American troops, in whatever direction they moved, had either to block one another's way massed in the narrow miry roads or else to deploy as best they could in the tangled undergrowth of the tropical forests; and came into the open close by the enemy's position only to expose themselves to a galling fire from foes lying unseen and protected. They had no support from artillery; each position they attacked had to be taken by cool, dogged assault; but the thing was congenial to their spirits, and was done with the steadfast pluck and the unfaltering audacity of men who did not know how to fail or turn back. The general officers who planned and ordered the movements knew, it presently turned out, neither the topography of the country nor the exact position and strength of the enemy;

but the men and their immediate commanders made all mistakes good and took what they found. On the 2d the American lines were still further advanced, and an assault by the Spaniards was repulsed. On the 3d General Shafter summoned the commander of the town to surrender; but General Toral had received reinforcements from the east and refused.

That same day the Spanish admiral, fearing himself trapped where he lay, put suddenly to sea, hoping by forcing his craft to their speed to run down the coast to the westward and show the American commander his heels before the blockading fleet could close upon him. But the first glimpse of his smoking funnels in the channel brought the fleet in the offing to the chase. The commander-in-chief was for the moment away, in his flagship, upon an errand to the eastward; Commodore Schley was in immediate command of the blockade. It was Sunday morning a little before ten o'clock, and the men were at quarters for inspection. They sprang to the work of chase and battle with a cheer, and within eight minutes the ships within range had opened fire. Hardly a signal was needed. The Spaniards swung in order down the coast; the American ships followed from their places in instant succession, each captain selecting the Spaniard he could most speedily get within range of for target. The foremost and fleetest of the Spanish vessels was overhauled and forced ashore upon the rocky coast within four hours of its exit from the port; the vessels which followed her had been destroyed before the fight was two hours old. The American gunners, pouring in a fire constant, precise, overwhelming, had cut the fire mains or ignited the ready ammunition or sent destroying heat and ruin to the machinery of the craft they chased, and they were one after the other run aground, burning fiercely fore and aft. It took as gallant work to get their crews off and succor them in their desperate peril as it had taken

WILLIAM T. SAMPSON

to bring them to their sudden fate. Six hundred Spanish officers and men lost their lives, killed or drowned; more than seventeen hundred were taken off the burned and ruined vessels as prisoners.

Two weeks more and Santiago, with all the eastern posts and districts of Cuba, was in the hands of the

287

Americans. Reinforcements came in to General Shafter which swelled his numbers to 21,000, and a complete line of investment was drawn around the city. His guns had at last come up. Eighteen thousand women, children, and foreign residents were allowed to pass

WINFIELD SCOTT SCHLEY

through his lines before he opened siege fire; but when the bombardment did begin it came at intervals from the heavy guns of the fleet as well as from the batteries on the hills, and the end was inevitable. Negotiations for surrender were opened on the 12th, and on the 17th not only the town itself but also all the eastern posts were rendered up. On the 21st of July Major General Miles sailed from Guantanamo Bay with a small force

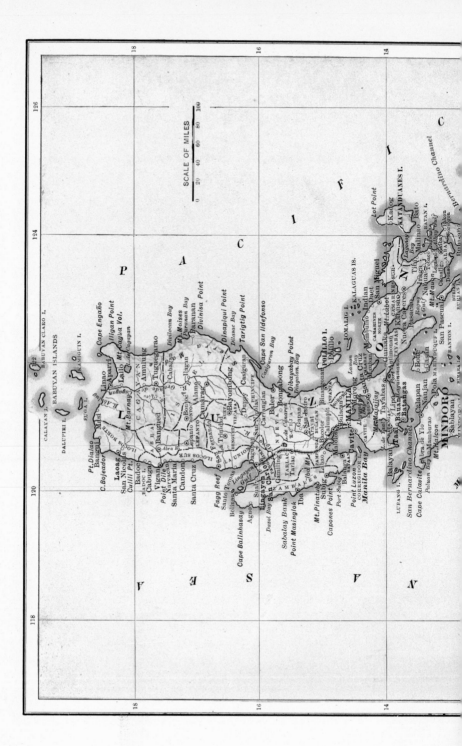

SCALE OF MILES

0   20   40   60   80   100

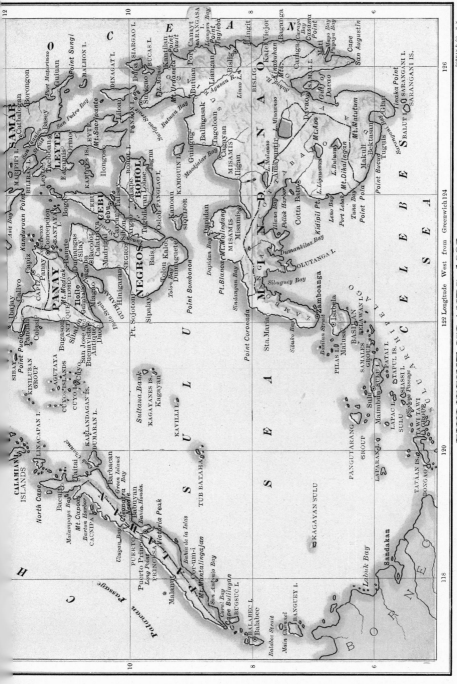

PHILIPPINE ISLANDS, 1902.

GEORGE DEWEY

v. —19

for Porto Rico. There he was joined by reinforcements out of the United States, and the southern and western portions of the island were taken possession of without opposition, the inhabitants even receiving the American troops with open enthusiasm. News of the arrangement of preliminaries of peace stopped all hostile movements before the occupation could be completed. On the 26th of July overtures of peace had been addressed by the Spanish government to the government of the United States through M. Cambon, the French minister at Washington; and on the 30th definite terms of peace were proposed from the same source. In August most of the troops in Cuba were hurried back to the United States to arrest the alarming progress of malarial fever, dysentery, and yellow fever among them; and the war seemed over,—except in the Philippines. On the 12th of August a peace protocol was signed at Washington.

In the Philippines Admiral Dewey had waited until troops should be sent which could capture Manila and take military possession of the islands. But he had not waited without armed allies. The Philippines, like Cuba, had been the scene of frequent rebellions against Spanish rule. Peace was, indeed, but a little more than four months old when Commodore Dewey received his orders from Washington to attack the Spanish naval force in eastern waters, and Emilio Aguinaldo, the one-time chief of the insurgents, was at hand, in Singapore, should the American commander wish to avail himself of his advice and aid. Commodore Dewey sent Aguinaldo word to follow him to Manila with all possible despatch, and he was given passage from Hong Kong on the American gunboat *McCulloch*. His influence with the people of the island of Luzon was well known. Young man though he was, scarcely turned of twenty-nine, they were his to command, so

WESLEY MERRITT

strong a hold had his frank manners, engaging interest in reform, and subtile power to turn men to his way of action taken upon them; and, for lack of troops from over sea, the American commander was willing

291

to supply him with arms and ammunition and put the men whom he should muster in a position to hold the country round about the city until the transports should come out of America and all things should be ready. To make such an arrangement was to play with fire. It was not clear, it could not be clear, what was to be done with the insurgent army thus set afoot again by American aid when the troops of the United States should arrive and the conquest of the islands be finally made.

Moreover, judicious lookers on wondered not a little to see the plans of the war so widened. Commodore Dewey had been commanded to destroy the Spanish fleet in the East; but he had not, so far as any one had heard, been told to take Manila and set an insurrection afoot in Luzon. It was significant that troops were at once hurried aboard the transports at San Francisco, —significant of the broadened scope and purpose of the war as viewed from Washington. It was not to stop with the relief of the Cubans. Troops were to be sent to the Philippines to take military possession of them. General Miles had been ordered from Cuba to Porto Rico. The power of the United States, once afield, was sweeping the island possessions of Spain into its sudden empire on both sides of the world. By the 13th of August, the day after the peace protocol was signed at Washington, all things were ready for the hostile movement at Manila and the place was easily taken by the American troops, Aguinaldo's forces looking on and doubting their part in the venture. When the peace commissioners met at Paris in the autumn to frame their final agreements, the United States demanded and got all that their arms had touched: Cuba for the

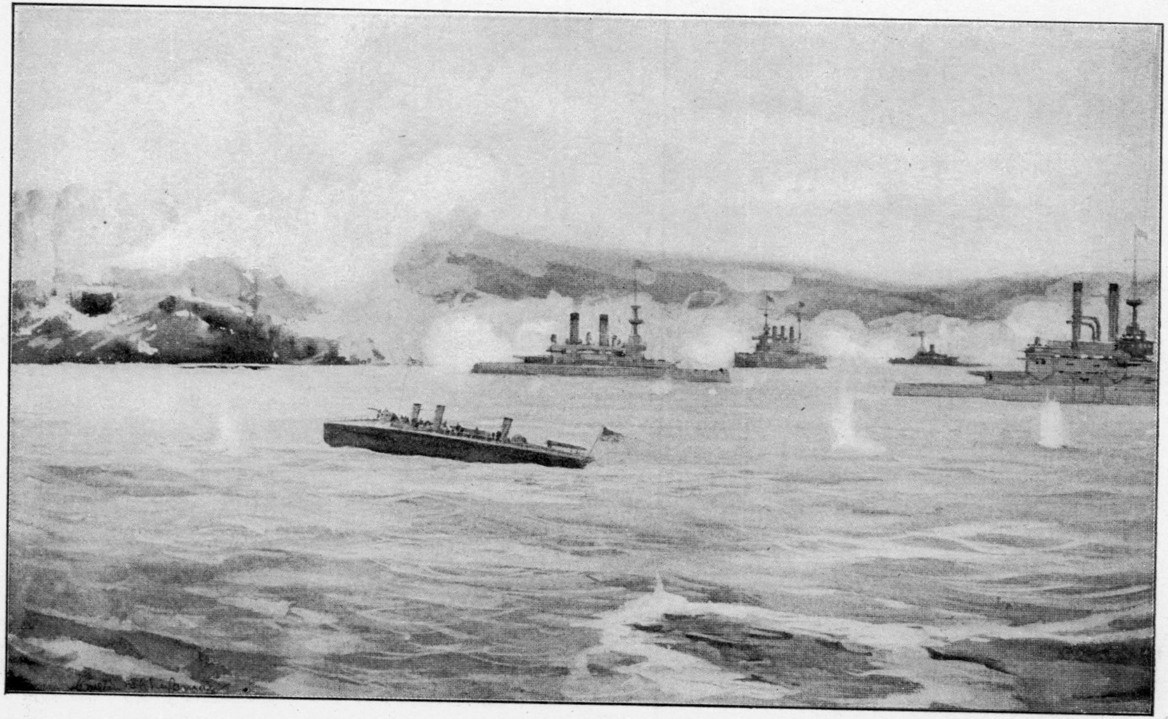

THE BOMBARDMENT OF SAN JUAN, PORTO RICO

FORT AND EARTHWORKS, CAVITÉ, SILENCED AND CAPTURED BY
ADMIRAL DEWEY

Cubans, Porto Rico and the Philippines, and the tiny
island of Guam by the way, for their own possession.
While the armies of the United States still lay with their
lines drawn about Santiago (July 6, 1898) a joint resolution had passed the two houses of Congress which
provided for the annexation of the Hawaiian Islands
to the United States and consummated the revolutionary
process to which Mr. Cleveland had for a little while
given pause.

Of a sudden, as it seemed, and without premeditation,
the United States had turned away from their long-
time, deliberate absorption in their own domestic development, from the policy professed by every generation of
their statesmen from the first, of separation from the

embarrassing entanglements of foreign affairs; had given themselves a colonial empire, and taken their place of power in the field of international politics. No one who justly studied the courses of their life could

EMILIO AGUINALDO

reasonably wonder at the thing that had happened. No doubt it had come about without premeditation. There had been no thought, when this war came, of sweeping the Spanish islands of far-away seas within the sovereignty of the United States. But Spain's empire had proved a house of cards. When the American power touched it it fell to pieces. The government of Spain's colonies had everywhere failed and gone to hopeless decay. It would have been impossible, it would

295

have been intolerable, to set it up again where it had collapsed. A quick instinct apprised American statesmen that they had come to a turning point in the progress of the nation, which would have disclosed itself in some other way if not in this, had the war for Cuba not made it plain. It had turned from developing its own resources to make conquest of the markets of the world. The great East was the market all the world coveted now, the market for which statesmen as well as merchants must plan and play their game of competition, the market to which diplomacy, and if need be power, must make an open way. The United States could not easily have dispensed with that foothold in the East which the possession of the Philippines so unexpectedly afforded them. The dream of their own poet had been fulfilled,

"See, vast trackless spaces,
As in a dream they change, they swiftly fill,
Countless masses debouch upon them,
They are now covered with people, arts, institutions."

The spaces of their own continent were occupied and reduced to the uses of civilization; they had no frontiers wherewith "to satisfy the feet of the young men": these new frontiers in the Indies and in the far Pacific came to them as if out of the very necessity of the new career set before them. It was significant how uncritically the people accepted the unlooked for consequences of the war, with what naïve enthusiasm they hailed the conquests of their fleets and armies. It was the experience of the Mexican war repeated.

What they claimed was not, indeed, yet theirs in fact. A sullen dismay and discontent had come

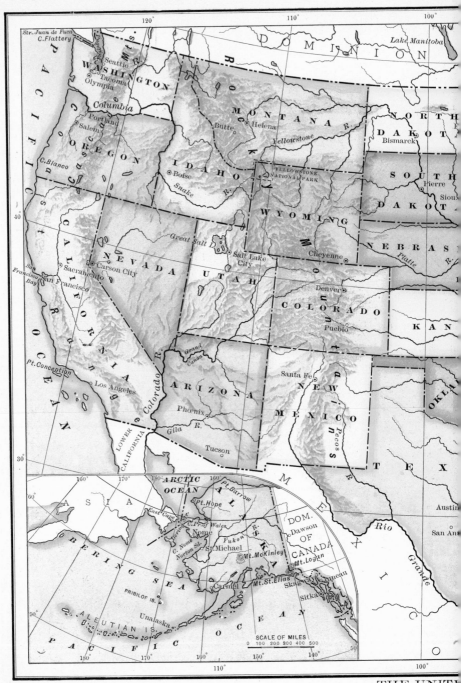

THE UNITE

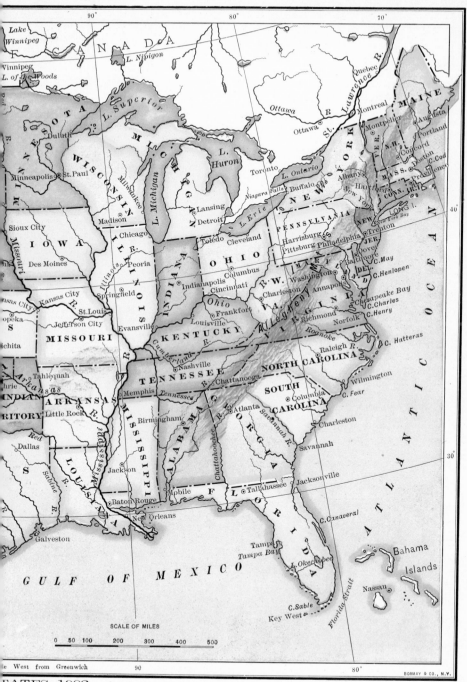

GULF OF MEXICO

SCALE OF MILES

0   50 100   200   300   400   500

le West from Greenwich   90°   80°

BORMAY & CO., N.Y.

TATES, 1902.

upon the men who served with Aguinaldo outside the American lines at Manila, and who did not clearly know whether they were allies or subjects. They had not taken up arms, they said, merely to make the Americans their masters instead of the Spaniards, but to make themselves free, and had deemed the Americans their allies in that undertaking. The American commanders had made them no promises, but they had seemed tacitly to accord them the place of allies, and their own hopes had drawn the inference. When they found that those hopes were to be denied them they took their cause into their own hands and set up the government as if of an independent republic with Agui-

TWO-STORY TENT OF COLORADO TROOPS, CAMP DEWEY, LUZON, PHILIPPINE ISLANDS

naldo as their president (September 29, 1898). In February, 1899, a dogged war of resistance began which it was to take the troops of the United States, recruited from season to season till their numbers reached quite 70,000 men, more than three years to bring to an end. But the end was visible from the beginning. As

THE U. S. S. OLYMPIA ON THE MORNING SHE LEFT MANILA WITH
ADMIRAL DEWEY ON BOARD

the presidential election of 1900 approached the Democratic party made as if it would stake its fortunes on an opposition to the "imperial" policy of the administration; but it found that the thoughts of the people did not run with it, and turned the force of its effort again, as four years before, to the silver question. Mr. Bryan was again made its candidate, against Mr. McKinley, whom the Republicans had renominated

Theodore Roosevelt

as of course, and it once more demanded in its platform the free coinage of gold and silver at the ratio of
sixteen to one. But no one feared now that it would
win upon that issue. The hopes and energies of the
country were turned in another direction, and Mr.
McKinley was elected without difficulty.

It was interesting to note with how changed an aspect
the government stood upon the threshold of a new century. The President seemed again to be always in the
foreground, as if the first days of the government were
to be repeated,—that first quarter of a century in which
it was making good its right to exist and to act as an
independent power among the nations of the world.
Now, full grown, it was to take a place of leadership.
The closing year of the century (1900) witnessed a great
upheaval of revolutionary forces in China. Insurgent
bands filled the country, the very capital itself, in protest against the presence and the growing influence
of the foreigner, and particularly the occupation of
new ports of entry by Russia, England, and Germany,
—the dowager empress, the real mistress of the kingdom, acting as their ally. The very legations at Peking
were invested in deadly siege by the insurgents; and
America, with the other nations whose representatives
were threatened, sent troops to their relief. America
played her new part with conspicuous success. Her
voice told for peace, conciliation, justice, and yet for a
firm vindication of sovereign rights, at every turn of
the difficult business; her troops were among the first
to withdraw, to the Philippines, when their presence
became unnecessary; the world noted a calm poise of
judgment, a steady confidence as if of conscious power
in the utterances of the American Secretary of State;

the new functions of America in the East were plain
enough for all to see. The old landmarks of politics
within the United States themselves seemed, meanwhile,
submerged. The southern States were readjusting
their elective suffrage so as to exclude the illiterate
negroes and so in part undo the mischief of reconstruction; and yet the rest of the country withheld its hand
from interference. Sections began to draw together
with a new understanding of one another. Parties
were turning to the new days to come and to the common
efforts of peace. Statesmen knew that it was to be their
task to release the energies of the country for the great
day of trade and of manufacture which was to change
the face of the world: to ease the processes of labor,
govern capital in the interest of those who were its indispensable servants in pushing the great industries of
the country to their final value and perfection, and
make law the instrument, not of justice merely, but
also of social progress.

INDEX

301

Butler, John, ii. 292.
Butler, Walter, ii. 292.
Byrd, William, ii. 100.

CABOT, GEORGE, iii. 186, 187.
California, ceded to United States, iv. 122; gold discovered in, iv. 135; government formed in, iv. 136; admitted to. Union, iv. 140.
Calvert, Cecilius, Second Lord Baltimore, i. 128, 130, 131, 133, 134, 135, 136.
Calvert, Charles, Third Lord Baltimore, i. 288, 339.
Calvert, George, First Lord Baltimore, i. 128, 131.
Calvert, Leonard, i. 188.
Cambridge platform, the, i. 198.
Camden, S. C., ii. 308.
Campbell, John, iii. 342.
Canada, Fenian raid in, v. 29, 30; fisheries of, v. 70.
Canals, iii. 243, 244, 266.
Canning, George, iii. 263.
Cape Cod, i. 86, 89.
Cape Fear, pirates at, ii. 44, 47.
Cape Henry, iv. 80.
Carleton, General Guy, ii. 256; iii. 15, 26.
Carlisle, John G., Secretary of Treasury, v. 189, 253.
Carolina :
Land grant of, i. 246; population (1663), i. 247; government of, i. 249–252; new charter of, i. 250; attacks Spanish at Florida, ii. 33.
"Carpet baggers" in the South, v. 46.
Carr, Dabney, ii. 183.
Carr, Robert, i. 226, 236.
Cartagena, attack on, ii. 71, 72.

Carteret, George, i. 239, 296, 298.
Carteret, Philip, first governor of New Jersey, i. 240, 242, 244, 295, 296, 298.
Cartier, Jacques, penetrates St. Lawrence, i. 18; fortifies Quebec, i. 19; ii. 6.
Cartwright, George, i. 226, 236.
Cass, Lewis, iv. 128.
Cathay, Columbus seeks, i. 2, 6.
Cavaliers in Virginia, i. 215, 216, 217.
Cedar Mountain, battle of, iv. 229.
Census, first of United States (1790), iii. 125; (1800), iii. 172; (1820), iii. 246; (1850), iv. 135; (1870), v. 66, 67; (1880), v. 166, 167; (1890), v. 199, 212.
Centennial Exhibition (1776), v. 120, 122.
Central Pacific Railway, completion of, v. 89.
Cerro Gordo, iv. 120.
Cervera, Admiral Pascual, commanding Spanish fleet at Santiago, v. 278.
Champlain, Samuel de, ii. 6, 8, 9.
Chapultepec, iv. 120.
Charles I., i. 100, 122, 124, 128, 173, 174, 175.
Charles II., proclaimed King in Virginia and New England, i. 213, 215; his letter to Massachusetts agents, i. 226; sends royal commissioners to Massachusetts, i. 226; gives New Netherlands to Duke of York, i. 229, 232.
Charles V., his empire and power, i. 20.
Charleston, S. C., settlement of, i. 254, 293; its social life, ii. 52, 54; negro slaves in, ii. 54;

v.—20

Continental Congress of, ii. 240.

Colonies :

At Jamestown, i. 37; at Quebec, i. 69; at Newfoundland, i. 69; at New Plymouth, i. 69, 90, 92, 95, 98; at Salem. i. 104; in Virginia, i. 110, 116; in Maryland, i. 131, 136; in Massachusetts, i. 138; in Connecticut, i. 138; on Long Island, i. 138; in North Carolina, i. 292; in South Carolina, i. 293, 294; in Pennsylvania, i. 304; in Savannah, ii. 64–67; effect of civil wars in England on, i. 171–181; restrictions on commerce of, i. 219–222; shipbuilding in, i. 221, 222; restrictions on trade in, i. 258, 261; government in, i. 290; conference of 1690 in, ii. 12; make war on New France, ii. 13; woollen manufactures in, ii. 19; effect of " Queen Anne's War " on, ii. 30; changes in 1721–1742, ii. 49–51; Scots-Irish settle in, ii. 51; party movements in, ii. 55, 56; English and French views of, ii. 101, 104; effect of Stamp Act on, ii. 134, 136, 137, 139.

Columbus, sets out to find Cathay, i. 1, 2; annotations in handwriting of, i. 3; seeks Asia and kingdom of Tartars, i. 4.

Commerce :

Between Southampton and Brazil, i. 32; Dutch, i. 70; Spanish, i. 70; English restrictions on colonial, i. 219–222; ii. 144.

Committee of correspondence, ii. 174, 175, 176, 178, 187.

Committee of inquiry on condition of the South (1871), v. 74, 76.

Common Sense pamphlet by Paine, iii. 91.

Commonwealth, the effect of, in Virginia, i. 215.

Comptroller of the Currency, the, iv. 252.

Concord, fight at, ii. 223, 225.

Confederacy, the Southern :

Beginnings of, iv. 199, 200, 271; States of, iv. 200, 208; capitol of, at Richmond, iv. 210; boundaries of, iv. 212; population of, iv. 249; social orders in, iv. 269, 270; organization of government of, iv. 271; provisional government of, iv. 272, 273; politics of, iv. 274; love for the Union in, iv. 276–278; constitution of, iv. 284; powers of President of, iv. 286; hopes of the leaders of, iv. 288; difference of opinions in States of, iv. 289; resources of, iv. 289, 290; scarcity of specie in, iv. 291, 292; paper money of, iv. 292; crops of, iv. 292; food and clothing in, iv. 293, 294; transportation in, iv. 295, 296; arms and munitions of army of, iv. 296–298; the army of, iv. 298–300; government of, iv. 301–306; conscription laws in, iv. 298, 304; financial measures of, iv. 304, 305; prisons of, iv. 307; dissolution of, iv. 311, 312; States of, after the war, v. 2–6.

Grangers, v. 124, 126.

Grant, Ulysses S.:

In Mexican War, iv. 219; volunteers in Union army (1862), iv. 219; occupies Cairo and Paducah, iv. 220; takes Fort Henry, iv. 221; at Corinth, iv. 221, 222; at Vicksburg, iv. 242; at Chattanooga, iv. 243, 248; at Lookout Mountain, iv. 248; made commander-in-chief, iv. 253; at Appomattox, iv. 258; his powers as general of the army, v. 37; appointed Secretary of War (1867), v. 54; elected President (1869), v. 57; his action against Ku Klux, etc., v. 75; his breach with Sumner, v. 80; re-elected President, v. 87; end of his administration, v. 96, 97; his refusal to send troops to Mississippi, v. 98, 99; public estimate of his administration, v. 112; as member of the firm of Grant & Ward, v. 167.

Grant & Ward, firm of, v. 167.

Grasse, Count de, in the Chesapeake, ii. 328; attacks British West Indies, iii. 4; defeated by Rodney, iii. 9.

Gray, Asa, iv. 80.

Great Meadows, battle of, ii. 83, 84.

Greeley, Horace, v. 80, 81; his advocacy of general amnesty, v. 82; nominated for President, v. 84; his death, 87.

Greenback party, the, v. 123, 145.

Greenback-Labor party, v. 154.

Greenbacks, government, v. 143.

Greene, Nathanael, ii. 314, 322, 323, 327.

Greene, Roger, i. 246.

Grenville, George, ii. 125, 130, 131, 132, 140, 145, 152.

Gresham, Walter Q., v. 248.

Grow, Galusha A., v. 134.

Guadaloupe, Hidalgo, iv. 122.

Guam, island of, v. 292.

Guantanamo Bay, v. 288.

Guiana, British, v. 245.

Guilford, i. 163.

Guiteau, Charles J., v. 156, 159.

HABEAS CORPUS, suspended, iv. 236; suspended in Southern States, v. 64; act authorizing suspension of, v. 75.

Hakluyt, Richard, i. 33, 42.

Half-breeds, political party of, v. 258.

Halleck, General Henry W., iv. 222.

Hamilton, Alexander:

His birth and breeding, iii. 64; his opinion on government, iii. 72–74; his *Federalist* papers, iii. 96; as Secretary of Treasury, iii. 103; his views on finance, iii. 108–110; his breach with Mr. Adams, iii. 158; as leader of the Federalists, iii. 170; his duel with Aaron Burr, iii. 178; his establishment of first United States bank, iv. 44.

Hamilton, Colonel, ii. 296.

Hampden, John, i. 174.

Hampton, Va., i. 52.

Hampton, Wade, v. 108.

Hampton Roads, iv. 237.

Hancock, General Winfield S., nominated for President (1880), v. 153.

Harper's Ferry, iv. 229; John

INDEX

318

La Salle, Robert, ii. 6.
Latin Union, states of, suspend coinage of silver, v. 144, 145.
Laud, Archbishop, i. 122, 124, 128.
Lee, Arthur, ii. 183, 185, 213.
Lee, Charles, ii. 221, 258, 288.
Lee, General Robert E. :
  His ancestry and breeding, iv. 225; his services in United States army, iv. 226; in Southern army, iv. 226; his sentiment against secession, iv. 226; at Chancellorsville, iv. 242; at Gettysburg, iv. 254; his surrender at Appomattox, iv. 258, 259.
Lee, Henry, ii. 298, 315.
Lee, Richard, i. 216; ii. 134, 176, 183, 185, 194, 241; iii. 23.
Leisler, Jacob, i. 329, 333, 335; ii. 11.
Leopard, the English cruiser, iii. 191, 192.
"Letters of a Pennsylvania Farmer," ii. 158.
Leverett, John, i. 207.
Lewis, William B., iv. 12.
Liberal Republicans, political party of, v. 84–86, 122.
Liberty, the sloop, ii. 160.
Liberty Song, the, ii. 205.
Lieber, Francis, iv. 80.
Liliuokalani, Queen of Hawaii, proposes new constitution, v. 240, 241; refuses general amnesty, v. 242.
Lincoln, Abraham :
  His debate with Douglas, iv. 182, 183; elected President, iv. 188; his birth and education, iv. 206, 207; calls for volunteers, iv. 208; calls extra session of Congress, iv. 214; his proclamation of blockade,
iv. 216; his policy regarding slavery, iv. 231; his proclamation of emancipation, iv. 232, 244, 247; his assassination, iv. 259; his address at Gettysburg, iv. 308, 309; his proclamation of amnesty, v. 2, 3; his second inaugural address, v. 4, 128, 131.
Lincoln, General Benjamin, ii. 278, 308; iii. 58.
Liquor, manufacture of, iii. 241.
Literature, early American, iii. 83, 84, 85, 87.
Little Big Horn, the, v. 102.
Livingston, Edward, iv. 53.
Livingston, Robert, iii. 182.
Locke, John, i. 250.
Log Cabin, the, iv. 86.
Long Assembly, the, i. 266, 269.
Long Island, i. 74; early settlements on, i. 160.
Longfellow, H. W., iv. 80.
Lookout Mountain, battle of, iv. 248.
Loudon, Earl of, ii. 90.
Louis XIV., plans to capture New York, i. 331, 332; violates treaty, ii. 28; death of, ii. 49.
Louis XVI., iii. 4.
Louisbourg, siege of, ii. 73.
Louisiana :
  Ceded by France to Spain, ii. 96; ceded by Spain to France, iii. 180; purchased by United States, iii. 182; made a State, iii. 238, 256; division of slavery in, iii. 254, 255; iv. 104; secession of, iv. 200; readmitted to the Union, v. 46; debt of (1868–1872), v. 48; Republican control in, v. 99, 100; returning board of, v. 100; struggle between Republicans

and Democrats in (1876), v. 106.

Lowell, Francis, iii. 240.

Lowell, James Russell, iv. 80.

Lowndes, William, iii. 212.

Lundy's Lane, battle of, iii. 223.

•

McClellan, General George B., iv. 212; organizes Army of the Potomac, iv. 224; driven back by Jackson and Lee, iv. 228; at Antietam, iv. 229.

McCormick, Cyrus H., iv. 73.

McCulloch vs. Maryland, iv. 19, 43.

Macdonough, Commodore Thomas, iii. 223.

McDowell, General Irwin, iv. 211, 228.

McEnery, Mr., v. 102.

Mackemie, Rev. Francis, ii. 41.

McKinley, William:

His tariff bill, v. 209, 210; on the silver question, v. 257; elected President, v. 262; calls extra session of Congress, v. 268; his character as leader, v. 272, 273; his re-election (1900), v. 298.

McKinley bill, the, v. 209, 210, 228.

Mackintosh, Captain, ii. 185.

McLane, Louis, iv. 51, 52, 53.

Madison, James:

As member of Continental Congress, iii. 67; speech on treaty with England, iii. 141; in *Federalist* papers, iii. 156; as Secretary of State, iii. 176; elected President, iii. 199; love of peace, iii. 204; effect of his administration, iii. 232, 234; drafts Virginia Resolutions, iv. 32.

Madison, Samuel, iii. 96, 110.

Magellan, Ferdinand, rounds South America, i. 10.

Maine, labor and vagrancy laws in, v. 21.

Maine, the United States battle-ship, v. 270.

Maine liquor law, iv. 164.

Manassas, iv. 224, 227.

Manhattan Island, i. 74, 96.

Manila, in Philippines, taken by United States, v. 276.

Manufactures:

In New England, ii. 51, 107, 108, 110; prohibition of, in the colonies, ii. 19, 102; of flax and hemp, iii. 124; of cotton, iii. 173, 240; of wool, flax, hemp, and silk, iii. 241; of liquor, glass, and furniture, iii. 241; of ships, iv. 239; society for promotion of, iv. 239.

March, Colonel, ii. 35.

Marco Polo, his journeys, i. 4, 5.

Marion, Francis, ii. 320, 325.

Marlborough, Duke of, ii. 30.

Marquette, Père, ii. 6.

Marshall, John, iii. 146, 163, 166; iv. 18, 19.

Mary, Queen, i. 80.

Maryland:

Founded by Lord Baltimore, i. 128; land grant of, i. 130; first settled, i. 131; origin of name, i. 133; Act of Toleration in, i. 190, 195; Act of Toleration repealed, i. 195; rebellion in 1676, i. 288; laws in, i. 289, 290; overthrow of proprietary government in, i. 335; made a royal province, i. 339; Protestant revolution in, i. 339; accepts of Articles of Confederation, iii. 18; the conditions before accepting, iii. 48.

INDEX

Spotswood, a proclamation concerning, ii. 44; Lincoln's policy concerning, v. 5; government charge of, after the war, v. 17–28; effect of emancipation on, v. 18–20; Southern legislation regarding, v. 20, 21; constitutional convention of, at New Orleans (1866), v. 34; as voters in Southern States, v. 44; controlled by carpet-baggers, v. 46–47; their dominance in the South, v. 58.

Nelson, Horatio, iii. 189.

Netherlands, revolt of the, i. 30.

Nevis, island of, ii. 21.

New Amsterdam, i. 160; arrival of Stuyvesant at, i. 202; royal commissioners to, i. 227; character of settlers in, i. 231, 232; English rule in, 231, 232.

New Bermuda, i. 52.

New England, contrasted with Virginia, i. 217, 218; trade in, ii. 18; Articles of Confederation of, ii. 331.

New English Canaan, Morton's, i. 87.

New Hampshire Patriot, the, iv. 48.

New Haven:
Settled under Davenport, i. 162; joins United Colonies, i. 170; seeks redress from Dutch, i. 198, 200; included in Connecticut charter, i. 233, 234; settlers move to New Jersey, i. 243; Yale College established in, ii. 28; labor and vagrancy laws in, v. 21.

New Jersey:
Origin of name, i. 240; land grant of, from Duke of York,
i. 240; government of, by Carteret, i. 242; migration from Connecticut to, i. 243; first assembly of, i. 244; the "Concessions" of, i. 244; proprietary government in, i. 294, 300; division into East and West, i. 298, 299, 300; made again a crown colony, ii. 27; her delegates to convention (1786), iii. 62–64; ratifies the Constitution, iii. 78.

New Madrid, iv. 221.

New Mexico, ruins of, i. 16.

New Netherlands:
Named by the Dutch, i. 73; extent of, i. 73, 74; land grants to patroons in, i. 116, 117, 165, 166; trade opened to all in, i. 166; New Netherland Company, i. 73, 74; royal commissioners to, i. 227; given to the Duke of York, i. 229.

New Orleans:
French settled in, ii. 59; importance of, to United States, iii. 180, 181; included in Louisiana purchase, iii. 182; battle of, iii. 225; taken by Farragut, iv. 224; riot in (1866), v. 34; General Butler in, v. 47.

New Providence, buccaneers at, ii. 22; pirates at, ii. 44.

New York, city of:
Changed from New Netherlands, i. 230; seized by Leisler, i. 329–331; threatened by Frontenac, ii. 11; great sickness in, ii. 34, 35; negro plots in, ii. 40, 56; freedom of dissenters in, ii. 41; free-

renders to British commissioners, i. 229.

Succession of secretaries, the, iv. 1.

Suffrage, laws regulating (1790), iii. 120, 121, 271; changes in, iv. 4, 5, 6; in southern States after the Civil War, v. 24, 25, 74, 82; Reconstruction Act on, v. 36.

Sugar, monopoly of, by English, i. 220.

Sugar Act, the, ii. 207.

Sullivan, General, ii. 300.

Sullivan's Island, ii. 249.

Sullivan's raid, ii. 300.

Sumner, Charles:
His opposition to slavery, iv. 167; his speech in advocacy of granting the suffrage to colored men, v. 25; his interview with Andrew Johnson, v. 32; his breach with Grant, v. 80; his Civil Rights bill, v. 97, 98.

Sun, the New York newspaper, iv. 82.

Supreme Court, the, iii. 106; its decision on legal tender, v. 205.

Susquehanna River, i. 133.

Susquehannocks, slaughter of, i. 269.

Swedish settlements in America, i. 168, 204.

Swiss in North Carolina, i. 292.

TALBOT, RICHARD, Duke of Tyrconnel, i. 337.

Talleyrand, iii. 146, 149.

Tampa, Florida, United States troops at, v. 280.

Taney, Roger B., iv. 54, 176, 178.

Tarleton, Banastré, ii. 217, 319.

Tariff:
A protective, ii. 281, 282, 283; an issue between North and South, iv. 23, 34; Whig Act on, iv. 97; reduction in (1887), iv. 176; for Civil War, iv. 214; in Confederate Constitution, iv. 284; accumulation of duties (1880), v. 163; reduction of, v. 164; effect of, v. 189; the Cleveland message on, v. 191, 192; Reform bill of (1894), v. 227, 228.

"Tariff of Abominations," the, iii. 283.

Taunton, i. 165.

Taxation without representation, ii. 150, 151, 152.

Taxes, on tea, ii. 161, 162, 167, 185; on distilled spirits, iii. 137; war, iv. 251; in southern States after the war, v. 47, 48.

Taylor, Zachary:
In Mexican War, iv. 117, 118, 120; elected President, iv. 129, 130; advice to California and New Mexico, iv. 136; death of, iv. 140.

Tennessee, admitted to the Union, iii. 112; secedes, iv. 208; re-admitted, v. 28, 29.

Tenure of Office Act, the, v. 52, 53, 181; repeal of, v. 195.

Terry, General Alfred, v. 102.

Texas:
United States relinquish rights in, iii. 258; treaty of annexation with, iv. 102; becomes member of Mexican Union, iv. 105; independence of, iv. 105, 106; overtures for annexation to United States, iv. 108–110; admitted to Union, iv. 112; boundaries of,

INDEX

335

INDEX

THE END